MAKING
A GARDEN
MATTHEW WILSON

MAKING
A GARDEN
MATTHEW WILSON

Quadrille
PUBLISHING

Contents

Introduction

Just why would anyone want to make a garden? Why would they want to take a part of the planet and shape it, plant it and nurture it, enduring the pain of failure, suffering the trials and tribulations of the weather and investing not inconsiderably of themselves emotionally and, in some cases, financially too? After all, it's not as if we actually *need* gardens, is it? At least, not in the same way that we need a home to live in, food to eat or friends to talk to, perhaps.

Over the last two decades in my life as a professional gardener I have met hundreds of people for whom the making of a garden was every bit as important as the security of the four walls of the home. Not as essential, no, but absolutely as important because for them, as well as for millions of others, a garden is a mode of expression, a means of exploring the artistic merits of colour, form, texture and space in a way that is accessible (anyone with a garden can garden) and ever-changing, thanks to the interaction of the weather, the growth and death of plants and the waxing and waning of the seasons. It is this love affair with gardens that is at the heart of this book.

Over the last 10 months I have met six more couples for whom the making of a garden has become an all-encompassing preoccupation: the owners of the six gardens featured in Channel 4's *Landscape Man*. Each of the garden projects was on a grand scale, but otherwise they were as different from one another as could be – from a cliff top in Guernsey to a valley in Wales, a castle and formal grounds in Essex to a paddock carved into dramatic canyons and ponds in Devon. Some of our garden owners wanted to return to nature, grow vegetables and rear livestock or simply indulge themselves in an overwhelming love of flowers;

others wanted, in the very best way, to show off, to make a beautiful, impressive place for friends and family to enjoy. In some cases their financial commitments have been significant, in others almost nothing has been spent at all, but in every case the overwhelming desire to create something living, breathing and tangible has been the same.

What I have learned from my career to date and in particular over the last 10 months is that making a garden successfully, in terms of creating a beautiful outcome that is also fit for purpose, is far from an easy proposition – there are numerous pitfalls at every turn that are enough to sink seasoned professionals, let alone novices.

Making a Garden sets out to help you overcome, and ideally avoid altogether, the many costly and heart-rending mistakes that can befall the process of making a garden. It does so by taking you through the thought processes that are so important when considering what you want from your outdoor space, using the six gardens featured in *Landscape Man* to illustrate the many different and sometimes conflicting demands that are part of the process, allied with examples from my own experience. From there I take you into the visionary aspects of garden making, unpeeling the aesthetic elements that make up the whole and the various merits thereof. Finally the book looks at numerous examples of previously designed gardens, how they were put together, who for, and why.

I believe that the making of a garden, whether large or small, should always be a pleasure, one that has the potential to reward in ways that have a depth that few activities in modern life share. I hope that *Making a Garden* will help you to enjoy those pleasures more readily, and help map the route to a successful garden-making experience more clearly.

THOUGHT PROCESS

1

'All nature is but art unknown to thee'
Alexander Pope

Human beings are, by nature, ingenious yet practical animals. We strive to make our personal environment better by improving the way it works, either by acquiring the items that deliver an improvement or by designing something that fits the bill. Along with our natural inclination towards filling our lives with stuff, these factors form powerful motivators, driving everything from the acquisitive desire for a new car to the realisation that putting up a set of shelves would really help to solve a storage problem.

Collectively we are now more aware and appreciative of good design than ever before, as well as being far less willing to accept the shortcomings of bad design. The realisation that the 'perfect' position for the car steering wheel is also the one that happens to obscure the top half of the speedometer, causing constant craning to read the speed – this and a hundred other instances of design shortcomings contribute to the many irritations of modern living.

The golden rule of design is that form follows function but, when something really works, the partnership between the two is seamless. I have an ancient carpenter's plane bought by my grandfather. It's beautiful because of the warm glow of the rosewood handle, burnished with the patina of use and age, and the quality of the oil-blackened steel, crafted with as much care as a sportsman's rifle. In this very practical object, form and function live together perfectly, simply because of the quality of the design and the standard of the materials used.

And yet, despite our appreciation of really good design, we rarely apply the same principles to our gardens. Instead, gardens tend to evolve from the application of practical considerations rather than any overarching design. For example, a washing line is a prerequisite in most gardens and its dual requirements (a sunny, open spot and a decent length between two points) dictate its positioning, on the longest linear plane between the house and boundary fence. And once the washing line is in place, the realisation dawns that the constant to and fro to hang up the washing is creating a muddy track down the middle of the lawn, so a path is made of paving stones and the garden is entirely bisected. In time, the need for that great overspill of home storage, the shed, becomes more pressing. And what better place to put it than at the end of the path already constructed for access to the washing line?

The resulting garden isn't really a garden at all, just an open space equipped for practicalities – all function and no form. If plants do make it into the equation, they are relegated to the garden's fringes for fear of making it feel small. But it doesn't have to be like this. It is perfectly possible to accommodate practicalities and aesthetics in a garden, no matter the size. In fact, a designed garden will actually work better ergonomically, simply because it has been designed and all the requirements of the owners carefully considered and applied.

The key to achieving this happy balance between beauty and usability is to spend some time thinking through what you want from your garden: what elements simply *have* to be in it, how you intend to use it and how much time and money you want to spend on it – both creating it in the first place and thereafter. But you should also allow yourself to dream, taking inspiration from nature, other gardens or even seemingly unrelated elements: architecture, music or art. I've been inspired by items as disparate as a 1950s architecture poster and the front grille of a 1970s Lada car (the former inspired the layout for a whole garden, the latter the design of a timber fence partition) and am always looking to the non-garden world for inspiration in colour, form and style.

This chapter will act as your guide to the thought processes behind designing your garden in a way that fulfils as many of your needs and desires as possible. It also reveals how the owners of the six gardens in *Landscape Man* have dealt with the combination of practicalities, aesthetics, prevailing conditions and ethical considerations in order to make their own dream gardens come true.

Who and what is the garden for?

OPPOSITE Gardens have the capacity to be complete works of art, their creation and care requiring a blend of art, craft and graft that develop over time. The main outcome of a thoroughly considered thought process is that practicalities and beauty sit side by side and ensure that the garden is everything it can be.

This may seem to be the most obvious question of all, yet it is usually the one that isn't answered early enough in the design process. Quite simply, without a clear understanding of 'who' and 'what' the garden is for, it will be impossible to create an outdoor space that successfully meets your needs. It is the horticultural equivalent of contemplating buying a two-seat sports car when you have a family of six (though for some there might be an ulterior motive for doing just that!).

The answer to the 'who' part of the question may not necessarily be fixed, as circumstances can change. These need to be factored in: there is, after all, little point in planning a garden for two if you hope to become a family of three, or four, or five. The 'what' element will probably throw up a number of different answers as you will need to consider the many different roles you would like your garden to fulfil. Do you want to create a space for outdoor dining, an area for children to play, or simply a beautiful garden to look at, relax in and unwind? Because needs, tastes and interests change and develop over time, the answers to this question may not be fixed either. And in a living environment like a garden there is the not inconsiderable matter of plants growing and changing as well, all of which can affect quite fundamental aspects of the space – light levels, space,, outside views and so on – and how it can be used.

But there is no doubt that time spent thinking about what you really want from your garden is time well spent, considering such questions as how you currently use your garden and how that might change if the garden changed. These are exactly the kinds of questions you should expect a professional designer to ask you as part of the design process. Remember that, in taking all the many practical considerations into account, you should also allow yourself to dream a few dreams and take a few flights of fancy. After all, gardens are for dreaming too...

Accommodating children and pets

ABOVE My old cat Bruce seemed to have been bred for garden destruction. He would wait patiently for the beautiful flower heads of ornamental onions (*Allium*) to begin opening, before attacking each one in turn!

OPPOSITE Children love to get their hands in the soil, digging up worms and creepy crawlies and watching seeds they have sown grow into mature plants. Setting aside an area just for children to garden is a great way to make this happen.

Gardens form a vitally important connection between people and the environment. For children in particular, the garden is the place where they may experience, very likely for the first time in their lives, such exotic creatures as worms and bumblebees, the untrammelled joy of getting really, really muddy, and the little miracle that comes when a seed is sown and grows into a plant.

But designing a garden to accommodate the needs of children, with their love of playing, digging and running around can be challenging. The simplest way to achieve this is to give them an area of the garden that is theirs and theirs alone, to look after and tend. This might be a simple raised bed where a few veggies can be grown, or a big pot for rearing a monster sunflower. And if you want to really engage children with the outdoor environment then there are a couple of 'must haves'. A compost heap or wormery full of slippery, wriggly worms, will be enthralling to youngsters, as well as being a really good lesson in the responsibilities we have towards waste and recycling. A wildlife pond is an endless source of fascination – a miniature universe full of incredible animals – and can be made perfectly safe, even for the tiniest of toddlers. Setting aside even the smallest of spaces in the garden for your children will give them a sense of responsibility and ownership. Not only is this great fun for them, and hugely educational, it will then leave the rest of the garden free to be developed for the grown-ups.

Whilst it might be relatively easy to accommodate the needs of children in a garden, pets are a completely different matter. For one thing there is no reasoning with a bouncy, wilful moggy, and not much point in trying to encourage the use of a specific area of the garden as you might with a child. As a result, there will always be a compromise when one of the clients of a garden designer is four-legged, as it simply isn't possible to design out every challenge in the garden.

There are, however, a few practical things that can be done to help offset the worst that pets can do. Taking your dog for a walk, rather than just letting it loose in the garden, is an obvious one. If you do have to let the dog use the garden for when nature calls, it's perfectly possible to train it to use just one spot. There are also charcoal-based additives that can help to neutralise the acid in dog urine, which is the cause of yellow patches in lawns. Cats are a different proposition as they are almost impossible to train, but leaving aside an area of nice, loosely dug soil – in effect an outdoor litter tray – can help to encourage their use of a specific area for toilet purposes. And avoiding plants like catnip (*Nepeta* species), which is basically like cat LSD, is probably a good thing.

Outdoor dining and entertaining

OPPOSITE This garden has been designed with the focus squarely on outdoor dining, the small space dominated by the large timber dining table. There are some nice touches here: the repetition of colour in the blue tea light holders and cushions, as well as the form of simple, rectangular planters.

There is little point in having a garden if you never use it, and without doubt one of the best ways to use a garden is to spend time living in it, whether that be entertaining, alfresco dining, or simply sitting out and enjoying the elements. Applying thought to how to design the areas where these activities take place will ensure they work in the way you want them to. For example, if you want to sit out in the sun it makes sense to have seating on level ground in a sunny spot in the garden. It sounds obvious, but you'd be surprised how easy it is to get wrong. And if eating outdoors is a priority, tackling a few practicalities by applying thorough design principles will make it even more of a pleasure: outdoor lighting, a weatherproof electricity supply, a surface for food preparation and cooking and a waterproof cover to sit under will all help transform your garden into the most popular restaurant on the street.

An outdoor dining space can become the hub from which the rest of the garden radiates, as well as being a thing of beauty and interest in its own right. A seating area can become a focal point that draws the eye, while a path that is at heart a practical feature to take you from the back door to the shed can become a route through the garden that feels like a journey, rather than just a simple A to B. These elements usually form the bulk of the hard landscaping features in the garden, and are therefore the ones with the biggest costs attached, so getting them right is even more important.

RIGHT A bespoke seating area offers the opportunity to integrate the design of the garden with that of the seating. In this instance the shape of the circular seating and table is echoed in the clipped box balls, whilst the table itself sits in a circular paved area.

LEFT This simple dining area is made a little more special by raising the decked area, creating a step up and giving the space its own distinct 'flavour' from the rest of the garden.

No time to garden

OPPOSITE Designing a garden where the clients have no time at all to garden will inevitably have an impact on the balance between hard and soft landscaping, with the emphasis falling on paving and decks and the type of plants selected for comparative ease of maintenance.

Gardening is an interactive pastime that engages us on many different levels – sensually, intellectually and physically. Those of us who find ourselves trying to juggle busy lives can find this interactivity to be, on occasions, a little too demanding. And yet we still want to have an attractive garden just as much as those who have the luxury of more time to spend.

As a result, the time-poor gardener often ends up with a space that is largely ignored, before being tidied up from time to time with a few hastily bought plants, the results of frantic forays to the garden centre. Another supposed 'solution' (though it is anything but) involves laying the entire garden to lawn. This seemingly easy option will result in you having a garden that is not only horribly dull to look at, but also deceptively high in maintenance – all that grass will still need cutting, unless you want to end up with knee-high hay. Paving the whole space over, by contrast, is guaranteed to bring on advanced depression; surely we spend enough time looking at concrete and tarmac without having it fill our gardens?

The good news is that it is possible to have a beautiful garden that is relatively easy to maintain, though such a space requires more rather than less planning in order to be successful. Lawns are notorious for requiring lots of input to keep them looking good and many are much bigger than they need to be; if you only plan on using your lawn to set up a table and a couple of chairs for summer drinks then make it the appropriate size, or dispose of it altogether. A well-planned balancing of hard and soft landscaping materials can also help to keep maintenance to a bearable level, without creating something that looks like a concrete jungle. Whilst plants often strike fear into the hearts of 'non-gardeners', especially those with limited time on their hands, they only ever cause problems when they have been incorrectly chosen or badly cared for. There are tens of thousands of plants for every kind of growing condition that can happily thrive together, beautifying the garden whilst taking very little trouble to look after. In fact, there are a large number of plants that are so successfully adapted to specific situations that they can get by with no input whatsoever – no watering, feeding, spraying or anything else. Using structural plantings of largely evergreen subjects is another effective way of providing greenery with comparatively little effort, whilst avoiding seasonal plants in favour of those with greater longevity will help save time too.

Site considerations

ABOVE The area where you live will have a microclimate that has a direct impact on the types of plants you can grow. Repeated heavy frosts, extreme wet and cold or drought and heat each require a different palette of plants in order to garden successfully.

Whatever your ambitions for your garden, the climatic and cultural (growing) conditions of the site will have the biggest say in what you will actually be able to achieve. You might be dreaming of a lush, tropical garden but if you live on the side of a windy, exposed hill with almost no sun and regular winter frosts then the chances of your dream becoming a reality are slender to non-existent, as the growing conditions are simply not right for plants with big, soft foliage.

There's a lot to be learned from taking in your surroundings and looking at how other people garden in your area and what plants they use. You'll probably find, for example, that the plants on one side of your street vary from those on the other, as a consequence of the orientation of one side of the road being distinct from the other. There are plenty of clues in nature too, especially when it comes to pointers about soil type and growing conditions, as wild plants tend to be quite particular about where they will grow. A good wildflower book can help you to understand this better, and might even become the starting point for a great hobby; I like nothing better than nosing around in hedgerows looking at wildflowers.

The most important thing to realise is that there is no such thing as the 'average' garden, or 'average' conditions. A side return to a building in a busy city (like the one on the opposite page) will have a set of environmental conditions – wind exposure, desiccation, noise and chemical fume pollution – that are quite different from those someone gardening in a rural situation. And yet you may find they have share some unexpected similarities; perhaps that rural garden backs onto an expanse of field that is regularly sprayed with chemicals by a noisy tractor? What is certain is that it will save a lot of time, money and energy to spend time observing and getting to know the climatic conditions of your garden before you do anything else, rather than going to great efforts only to discover that everything is in the wrong place, or does not work with the conditions that exist in your garden.

Case Study *Guernsey*

RIGHT The growing conditions on Guernsey are typical of seaside locations. Persistent winds laden with salt spray, high light levels and changeable weather call for a very specific type of planting.

Climate and microclimate

BELOW The dappled shade of a deciduous tree in an otherwise sunny space can create a microclimate quite distinct from the rest of the garden: cooler, drier (thanks to the tree roots) and slightly more sheltered.

When considering your site, you should make gaining an understanding of the climatic conditions that are prevalent in your garden a priority. These conditions are a combination of the bigger climatic picture – rainfall, summer temperatures, degrees of frost in winter – along with the microclimate that exists in your garden. There's a distinction between the two, because the wider climatic conditions, the macroclimate, don't always translate down to what happens at garden level, which can be incredibly varied and specific, hence it being referred to as microclimate.

To begin understanding your garden's microclimate, start by asking yourself the question, 'What direction does my garden face?' North, south, east or west – this will have the biggest say on what you can grow because it will affect the amount of direct sunlight that falls on your garden. This in turn affects the temperature, which impacts on how quickly the soil warms up, when plants start into active growth and so on.

The physical built environment around a garden also influences the microclimate. A side return to a building might cause a funnelling effect of the wind, which in turn might have an adverse effect on any plants near the

side return, or make it an uncomfortable place to sit in. Solid walls can cause the wind to vortex or eddy, which is especially unpleasant if the wind picks up dust or soil.

And what about that most ubiquitous of features, the humble garden fence? A fence is, of course, designed to divide a space, and consequently its two sides face in opposite directions. Although the fence might be just a matter of a few centimetres wide, those two sides will have completely different compass aspects – if one side is south-facing the other is north-facing, if one faces west the other will face east. So within that very short distance two completely different microclimates will exist, which in turn means that what thrives on one side of the fence is unlikely to grow well on the other side, despite the distance between the two being so tiny.

The only way to really understand the conditions in your garden is to spend some time observing it. What you see might throw up some real surprises; an otherwise shaded garden may have an area that is in full sun through the middle of the day, for example. This information doesn't just influence the choice of plants you grow, but also the design of the garden – an area of full sun might be the perfect location for a seating or dining area, whilst a wall bathed in dappled sunlight might benefit from a change of colour to a more light-reflective hue. A heavily shaded spot where the frost sits during winter might not be a great place to sit out in, but could be brought to life with the planting of some late-flowering grasses, which look great all through winter and are at their absolute best when rimmed with frost.

ABOVE Knowing where the sunniest, most sheltered spot in your garden is can help to inform where you position a seating or dining area to make the most of the conditions you want to enjoy most.

The soil in your garden

Although it isn't especially exciting stuff at first glance, without soil there wouldn't be much life on Earth. And although an intricate knowledge of the ecology of soil isn't really essential in order to design a successful garden, a basic understanding is most certainly needed, as is an appreciation of how to manage soil to get the best out of it.

The important stuff to remember is this. Healthy soil is made up of mineral matter (in effect ground-down rock), which comprises roughly 50–60% of the whole, and organic matter at around 5%. Between the two, these form the solid part of the soil. The remainder is a roughly equal mix of air and water, both of which are vital for keeping the soil healthy and ensuring good plant growth. In order to keep soil healthy, and therefore the plants that grow in it happy and flourishing, these component parts need to be maintained at their relative amounts.

Soil types vary from heavy, wet clay to light, fast-draining sand, and the nature of the soil in your garden will affect what you should put in it to improve it for growing, as well as the type of plants you should use. The soil in your garden will also be more or less acidic or alkaline and this is measured using the pH scale. This has as big an effect on what kind of plants you can grow as the climatic conditions and soil type, as some plants are lime-haters, others acid-lovers and so on.

Soil types are incredibly variable, sometimes changing characteristics within a matter of metres. But providing you have a basic understanding of the soil characteristics in your garden you should be able to start making some improvements to the growing conditions. Whilst soil improvement is a massive subject, there are some broad rules for the most common soil types.

Sandy and silt soils

Sandy soils drain well and are quick to warm in spring. They are nice and light to dig and cultivate, but can be harder to 'improve' than heavier soil, as nutrients often wash through the top soil. Consequently they are less suited to plants requiring nutrient-rich soils and better suited to plants from hotter and/or dryer environments. Heavyweight soil improvers such as farmyard manure are ideal for light, sandy soil and can be dug in or, better still, applied to the surface as mulch every year, in spring and autumn.

Clay soils

Clay soils can be hard work; heavy and wet in winter like a wobbly blancmange, hard as concrete in summer. Clay soils tend to be hard to cultivate and poorly drained, which can cause plants to rot off in the ground, or 'drown' in the wet soil. But clay can be harnessed, so long as it's dug at the right time when the soil is neither too wet nor too dry, and the correct soil improvers are used – grit to improve drainage and lightweight organic matter such as an ordinary garden compost or spent mushroom compost to improve structure.

Soil basics

Whatever type of soil you have, there are a few basic rules that should be adhered to in order to ensure that it stays in good condition and is therefore the best it can be for growing plants in. You should

LEFT The soil conditions in the garden at Hedingham Castle in Essex – moist but well-drained acidic loam – are suitable for growing ericaceous (acid-loving) shrubs such as *Pieris*, which would not grow successfully in alkaline soil.

only ever cultivate soil when the conditions are suitable, which means avoiding periods when the ground is very wet, frozen or extremely dry. Digging in dry weather will simply remove whatever moisture is left, while any amount of disturbance or weight put onto wet or frozen soil can spoil its underlying structure, as well as the vital balance of air porosity that helps to keep it healthy.

To keep feeding the soil with the organic matter it needs, apply a mulch every spring and/or summer to the surface of the soil. This will help to keep moisture in, suppress weeds and feed the soil as, over time, the organic matter gets drawn down by soil-dwelling animals, in particular earthworms. Applying organic matter to the surface in this way also helps to reduce the amount of digging required, too much of which is actually a bad thing for the soil as it can disrupt and kill soil animals and cause problems to the soil's structure.

CREATING A GARDEN FROM SCRATCH

Clive and Debbie Morris have taken a long time to set down roots in a place they can truly call home. Their business in property development has meant that they have tended to spend a limited time in any of their homes, instead preferring to improve the quality of the property before selling up and moving on. As a consequence, they have never really engaged with the idea of a garden being something to experience and nurture. They bought their current home – a large detached property in Suffolk including a 24-acre garden that was once part of the Ickworth Estate – with the aim of improving it and selling it on. However, within a very short space of time they had fallen in love, both with the house and, more specifically, the garden.

Clive and Debbie's inspiration for their garden has part come from Ickworth Estate itself, a formal Italianate garden with Victorian additions. They see it as providing a place for family and guests to enjoy and be entertained in, as well as establishing a suitable setting for the house. In Clive's words, their aim is to put the life back into what had become a dead heart.

To help achieve their dream, the Morris's have engaged RHS Chelsea Flower Show gold-medal-winning designer Thomas Hoblyn. His plans for the garden are in essence a modern take on the classical landscaped garden estate. These include using structural plantings (such as avenues of trees) to emphasise existing vistas to the surrounding countryside or create new ones; a modern take on the classical rose garden; as well as the creation of a Victorian stumpery – a grotto made from the stumps of felled trees planted with ferns and other shade-loving plants – inspired by one at Ickworth.

But by far the most ambitious of the Morris's plans is the proposed transplantation of a complete RHS Chelsea Flower Show garden, which Thomas has designed for the 2009 Show. Chelsea Show gardens are impressive, expensive installations aimed at showing off a designer's skills, just as the big fashion shows of Paris, Milan and London showcase the talents of fashion designers. But what they aren't designed to do is last more than a week, the length of time over which the show takes place. Dismantling this show garden, recreating it in Clive and Debbie's garden and reinterpreting it to work, long term, in a very different space is a real design challenge and takes the idea of creating a garden from scratch to a new level!

ABOVE Forming an axis from the house out into the countryside beyond, a hornbeam avenue (1) will eventually link with an avenue of poplar and a garden rotunda. Adjacent to the main terrace of the house is a mixed rose and perennial garden (2) that is linked to Thomas Hoblyn's Chelsea Flower Show garden (5), the culmination of the formal garden area, by a simple area of meadow grasses and wildflowers (3). The existing small area of woodland has been improved with thinning out, new plantings and the creation of a stumpery garden (4).

The formal garden

Historically, a formal garden is one based around geometry: straight lines, often interlocking, that frame important vistas or focal points; neatly ordered and edged beds, frequently planted with a restrained palette; as well as the liberal use of structural planting in the form of trees, shrubs and hedges.

As Western garden and landscape design developed over the centuries, it was subject to the influence of art, poetry, science, architecture and social developments too. During the Elizabethan era the comparative stability of the country affected the architecture of grand houses to such an extent that it also changed the way gardens were designed. No longer needing fortifications or castellation as a means of defence, grand houses could instead be built with big windows. which were ideal for looking down onto a garden from and led to a rise in interest in the Knot Garden: a formal, symmetrical arrangement of low, clipped hedges surrounding plantings of fragrant herbs, designed to be viewed from above. There was a practical aspect to these gardens too – the herbs could be cut and strewn on the floor to suppress the widespread unpleasant odours that wafted around.

From the late 17th century, landscape design theory began to be increasingly informed by the experience of the 'Grand Tour', the tradition by which young men of means would travel Europe as an educational rite of passage, taking in important historical sites and developing their appreciation of classical and renaissance art. As well as accumulating knowledge, these young men would collect works of art and commission new works as copies, including garden statuary and furniture such as balustrades, columns and pillars – grand sculpture that demanded a suitably grand garden setting.

In modern times, as designers have felt less constrained by tradition, the factors that define formal and informal gardens have become increasingly blurred. In the contemporary sense, the notion of a formal garden is more to do with borrowing stylistic cues relating to geometric precision, framed views and vistas and architectural features, rather than an attempt to re-create a classical formal garden experience in its entirety. The design for Clive and Debbie's Suffolk garden includes a number of these classic formal garden features, such as tree avenues and rose gardens, which have either been updated or reinterpreted for use in a contemporary garden.

'In the contemporary sense, the notion of a formal garden is more to do with borrowing stylistic cues ... than an attempt to re-create a classical formal garden experience in its entirety'

LEFT This photograph of the pleached hornbeam avenue under construction shows how heavy and impermeable to water the heavy clay soil in Clive and Debbie's garden is. The excavated trench shown is being prepared for a new hard path between the hornbeams.

ABOVE The completed pleached hornbeam avenue, showing the timber frame onto which the hornbeams have been trained. This frame will stay in place for up to five years, whilst the hornbeam establish, before being removed.

Using trees in the garden

OPPOSITE Clive and Debbie's greatest enthusiasm is for trees – the pair have planted numerous long-lived hardwood trees such as oak (top left and middle right) to screen views of a nearby road and form avenues, clumps and woods, and have also invested a lot of effort in preserving the garden's existing old trees such as *Cedrus atlantica* (bottom right), which has been inoculated with beneficial fungus to help prolong its life. Where old trees have died (bottom left), they have been left standing to benefit the many animals that live in or feed on dead timber.

We humans have a bit of an odd relationship with trees. On the one hand we admire them and are somewhat in awe of their presence, longevity and, on occasion, massiveness. On the other we resent them for blocking the light from our windows, fear their questing roots lest they end up causing our homes to subside and curse the seasonal chore of leaf collecting. But to see trees in this way is to miss the point, which is that they are utterly and completely amazing organisms. They manufacture oxygen, filter pollution, provide homes for wildlife and can produce food, building materials and fuel. And the fact that they can do all of these things whilst putting up with the kind of abuse that we mete out on them – digging up their roots, hacking into their branches and mutilating their trunks – makes them all the more astounding.

In Clive and Debbie's garden, trees are used in a number distinct ways and, though the size of their garden is such that the numbers and size of the trees involved is pretty big, the same rules apply in locations where space is at a premium and when using much smaller-growing trees in very limited numbers or singly. Around the fringes of Clive and Debbie's garden, large clumps of big forest trees are used to screen elements of the surrounding landscape – other properties adjoining the estate as well as a road that runs in the view line of one of the boundaries. The tree clumps are grouped in such a way as to break up, but not entirely block, the line of the horizon. This important lesson applies to small gardens too. If you try to conceal something with a block of plants, you'll only emphasise the shape of the object you're trying to hide, whereas if you break up the outline with different shapes it should successfully disappear.

Elsewhere in Clive and Debbie's garden, trees are used not to hide things but to really show stuff off. To one side of the house an axis of trees extends out into the garden and through an adjoining paddock. Initially formed of an aerial hedge of pleached hornbeam (*see page 31*), the line is then extended with an avenue of poplar out to a pair of mature oaks which flank a large rotunda. The aim is the equivalent of shouting 'look at me', as the combination of tree avenues guides the eye towards the rotunda. This principle of using plants for emphasis, either to draw attention to a particular feature inside or outside the garden is particularly effective and can be applied to a garden of any size.

A MOST AMBITIOUS GARDEN TRANSFORMATION

ABOVE Keith and Ros Wiley bought a four-acre paddock in 2004 and have set about transforming it into a very different kind of garden, with a limited budget and largely without additional help.

Keith and Ros Wiley have spent a lifetime making gardens. For 25 years Keith worked as Head Gardener of a public garden in Devon, before leaving to create his own garden from a four-acre grazing paddock nearby. As well as making a garden, Keith and Ros needed to build up their nursery business on the same site in order to make a living. The first three years were pretty tough. Between them the pair took almost no time off; toiling away seven days a week to make the garden and build up the nursery business, whilst living onsite in a fairly basic timber cabin. Ros, a talented landscape artist, hardly picked up a paint brush during this period, spending all her time weeding and potting up plants instead.

Creating a garden from scratch can often be a difficult endeavour, but Keith's approach to making this garden has added to that challenge enormously. The paddock that Keith and Ros purchased was a perfectly decent field with level ground and a gentle slope towards the south – exactly the kind of conditions that most people would choose. However, instead of taking advantage of the prevailing conditions and working with them, Keith decided to completely transform the topography of the site. Using an excavator, he has carved out canyons, created pools of water and hillocks of soil, some over 4 metres tall. The result is quite extraordinary; plants sweep up and down over the hillocks, through which winds a network of paths.

In the centre of all this Keith has created a courtyard garden, flanked by block-built walls that have been rough rendered with a coloured plaster in the style of a Mexican *hacienda*. Inside the courtyard, the space is divided into four roughly equally sized beds, separated by a cruciform path with a huge stone trough acting as a centrepiece. Here Keith plans to create an exuberant planting scheme based around four 'groves' of large pineapple trees (*Cordyline* species).

To top it all off, Keith has excavated two huge ponds that extend along the whole southern boundary of the garden. The trouble is, Keith and Ros have very little help or funding with which to make all of these ambitious plans come to fruition, and as well as trying to complete the garden – which they need to open to the public to help support their business – they also have the added challenge of trying to keep their nursery running at the same time.

ABOVE The major design feature of Keith and Ros's garden is a series of ponds and bog gardens (1) that are linked by narrow streams and waterfalls and fed entirely by rainfall. A planned summer house (2) will provide a vantage point from which the ponds can be enjoyed, while new paths (3) created around the ponds allow the richly-planted fringes and banks to be glimpsed close up. A series of bridges (4) provide crossing points over the water features as well as additional structural interest.

The naturalistic garden

ABOVE Keith's greatest enthusiasm is for flowers, especially the overwhelming displays of wildflowers seen in nature, the impression of which he has sought to bring back to his own garden in Devon.

The term 'naturalistic garden' is a rather loose one that has come to prominence in recent years, with the upsurge in interest in gardens that are planted in tune with nature and which consequently need less frequent intervention to keep them healthy and looking good. In design terms there are no rules that apply specifically to a naturalistic garden – it is more an ethos than a style – and so a naturalistic garden could in principle be created within the context of formal design principles, or just as easily be a wild, woolly, unplanned space.

Although all gardeners have to exert a certain element of control over nature to keep their gardens in shape, the naturalistic gardener will go to great lengths to ensure they have a thorough understanding of the soil type and microclimate in their garden before choosing the appropriate plants for those conditions, rather than just buying plants they like the look of, planting them and hoping for the best. A naturalistic garden will, by and large, use little or no additional water for irrigation, minimal or zero pesticides and no fertiliser. The plants selected will tend to be very natural-looking too, as they will usually be wild species (not necessarily native to this country but native to somewhere on the planet) or hybrid plants that share most of the characteristics of their wild parents – nectar and pollen richness for example. As a consequence of management and plant selection, a garden made in this way will often be buzzing with wildlife and tend to look more a part of the landscape than something imposed upon it.

> **'There are no rules that apply specifically to a naturalistic garden – it is more an ethos than a style'**

When Keith started making his naturalistic garden, his aim was to create a facsimile of the wild landscapes that have influenced him and his style of gardening for years: the panorama of European Alpine meadows, the bleak beauty of the Mojave Desert and Death Valley in California, and the bright blossoms of the South African Fynbos. What Keith is attracted to in all of these wild places is their vast array of flowers, the blooms of which often last no longer than a few weeks but arrive in a great flush of colour that has the power to overwhelm the senses. By creating hillocks and canyons for these plants to grow on, their colourful flowers are immediately brought up to head height and so can be looked at directly, recreating that early childhood sensation of being lost amongst a multitude of flowers.

BELOW Comprising of canyons and valleys carved from the flat field with an excavator, Keith and Ros's garden is full of flowers and buzzes with wildlife. Despite the poor sub-soil, consisting of shards of stone mixed with clay, there is plenty of nutrition here for growing a wide variety of plants.

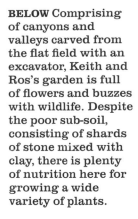

Ponds

OPPOSITE Ponds don't just look good, reflecting light, sky and the plants around them, they are also hugely important for wildlife; providing food and habitat and consequently attracting a wide range of species to the garden.

One of the key features of Keith and Ros's garden is a series of ponds that run along the bulk of the garden's southern boundary. Although these aren't technically big enough to be classed as lakes (the definition of which is a body of water with a surface area greater than one acre) they are no shrinking violets, the largest being 25 metres long, 5 metres wide and 2 metres deep. They form the culmination of the garden as an experience, the final big surprise in a garden that has more than most. They also serve a practical purpose too, with Keith planning to use them as informal reservoirs, to provide irrigation water for the nursery and garden, as needed.

While a garden pond may seem a fairly innocuous feature – a simple hole in the ground filled with water and ornamented by a few plants – it really is anything but. A well-designed and executed pond, whatever its size, will begin to attract wildlife within days of being built. First to arrive are usually passing birds, lured by the opportunity for a bath and a drink. The pond's wet margins also provide plenty of mud; the principal building material from which barn swallows and house martins make their nests.

'A well-designed and executed pond, whatever its size, will begin to attract wildlife within days of being built'

Once the water starts to settle and naturalise (which is pretty soon if the pond has been responsibly filled with rainwater rather than from the tap), creatures that live in or on the water will appear – water boatmen with extended legs like oars to propel them across the water surface, whirligig beetles that spin endlessly and seemingly uncontrollably, as well as myriad tiny insects and bacteria that help to keep the water balanced.

In time, if the pond has been planted with the correct density of plants to keep it healthy (a mixture of floating, submerged oxygenating plants as well as water lilies and plants that provide shelter around the water's edge) then even more exciting and exotic-looking creatures will show up: insects such as dragonfly larvae, equipped with vicious mouth parts designed for snapping up prey, as well as great diving beetles that appear as if from nowhere to scour the water's murky depths.

Starting from scratch versus taking on an existing garden

OPPOSITE
Sometimes inheriting an existing feature might seem like a double-edged sword: the benefit of a mature feature is often welcome, but how do you go about including it in a new design? In this instance an existing mature tree has become a central feature in a new design, from which the rest of the garden now radiates.

For an enthusiastic gardener the idea of taking on an empty blank canvas of a space and, from it, creating a new garden, is an exciting one full of promise. For the uninitiated and inexperienced, however, it has the potential to feel like an overwhelming challenge. Starting a garden from scratch offers as many opportunities as it does potential pitfalls. On the one hand, there are none of the limitations caused by the sorts of features found in a mature garden. Nor is there the temptation to live with something that you just know is in the wrong place, like a patio or a path, simply because it is already there and it would be too expensive, difficult, or time-consuming to move it.

An empty space can throw up its own set of distinctive problems, however. There is nothing to give a garden any sense of being rooted in a new garden, nothing with scale to provide presence or hide unsightly neighbouring structures. The only way to counteract this, if there is a need to do so quickly, is with hard cash – buying in maturity in the form of big trees and shrubs or garden structures with scale. There can also be problems that arise from the conditions on the site: a newly built property (one of the most common instances where a new garden is taken on) can often have garden 'soil' that is little more than builders' rubble. Often there is little to do but remove the top 30cm or so of soil and replace it with bought-in topsoil, an expensive and messy operation that doesn't always solve the problem, as bought-in soil often doesn't match the prevailing conditions in the area, and can be of poor quality too.

A pre-existing garden is likely to have at least a couple of mature plants, which can give the garden a sense of presence, and may well have other useful features such as seating areas, a garden shed and so on. But what if none of them are to your taste? What if the one tree in the garden is patently in the wrong place? How do you go about choosing which plants to save and which ones to remove? The liberating freedom of the blank canvas can seem a blessing by comparison, but when tackling a mature garden, it is the pre-existing features themselves that should be savoured and built upon. With a bit of thought (and a little work) it might be possible to revamp existing hard landscaping features like paths and patios and give them a new lease of life, whilst that one mature tree in the centre of the garden could, with careful pruning, become a lighter, more open feature around which the new garden pivots.

PLANNING THE PERFECT SPACE

ABOVE Filming on location at Anne and Geoff's garden in Sussex by the tennis court: a part of the garden that was often a source of contention (*see page 44*). After much discussion between Ann, Geoff, myself and their designer, the court was eventually turned into a wildlife pond.

Anyone searching for a garden with real potential could do worse than heed the estate agent's mantra of 'location, location, location'. Anne and Geoff Shaw had been looking for a property in the area of the South Downs in Sussex for almost five years before purchasing a run-down and unloved old house and dilapidated garden in a wonderful setting with spectacular views. Having spent so long searching for the right property, they are understandably anxious to create a great garden – but to do so they must first overcome some pretty big challenges.

Great views often come at the price of exposure to the elements. Anne and Geoff's garden is no different in this respect, being located at the top of a ridge overlooking a valley. Careful thought will therefore be needed to ensure that the garden is designed in such a way as to allow them to enjoy the beautiful scenery without having to retreat into the house whenever the wind blows. The soil in the garden is another problem: heavy clay that will need to be skilfully managed if anything is to be made to grow in it.

But the biggest hurdle the pair must overcome are the local planning rules. Anne and Geoff's home is very old, with parts of it dating back to 1650. As a consequence, the local planning officers are keen to ensure it is developed sensitively, and their scrutiny doesn't stop with the house. The curtilage of the garden – the clearly defined area associated with the house that has always been gardened as opposed to farmed – is very obviously marked by old flint walls that appear in ancient tithe maps of the site. Anne and Geoff have engaged garden designer Ian Kitson to create a plan which includes sweeping, curving walkways and dramatic sunken gardens, along with wildlife pools and wildflower meadows. Crucially, however, this plan proposes alterations to the curtilage.

Altering such a historically important feature as curtilage isn't something to be entered into lightly, especially in somewhere like the South Downs: a pocket of natural beauty in the busy southeast of England so precious that they were awarded National Park status in 2009, which brings with it much stricter planning regulations to protect the landscape from inappropriate or damaging development. Anne and Geoff will therefore have to rely on Ian to help lead them through the tricky business of making a beautiful garden on a site that is both physically challenging and is subject to the approval of the local authorities' ever-watchful eye.

ABOVE The old tennis court (1) has now been redesigned into a wildlife pond that is the highlight of the new design. It features a large timber deck which spans the water, widening enough to include a seating area before 'diving' into the water close to a small wildlife island. The sunken garden (3), in front of the house is another significant new feature, the walls dressed with napped flint in the local vernacular style. A previously steep level change (2) has been graded out using spoil from the excavation of the sunken garden, whilst beyond the old boundary wall a wildflower meadow (4) helps to blend the garden with the wider countryside.

Hide-and-seek

OPPOSITE The garden at Anne and Geoff's home was largely overgrown and near derelict when they bought the property, with just the odd stone sculpture (top right) and a few plants (middle right and bottom left) as a reminder of its gardened past. Designer Ian Kitson's plans for the garden have needed alterations along the way to take into account planning, budgets and permissions. For example, the old tennis court (top left), which was originally destined to be resurfaced and refurbished, has instead been turned into a wildlife pond.

Every garden has a feature or features that we wish we could hide away. Often it is the practical elements of a garden – the wheelie bin, the rotary washing line or the garden shed – the necessary parts of the 'working' aspect of a garden, which are amongst the most aesthetically challenged. And yet, in just the same way as a kitchen or a bathroom, this is a space that has to do things. Anne and Geoff's garden is blessed with two great natural characteristics: it is in an elevated position, and it has fantastic views to the surrounding landscape of the South Downs. But right in the way of the most important view from the house – the one that is seen from the entire rear aspect of the property – a previous owner has built a tennis court.

When compared with more prosaic items such as rotary washing lines, a tennis court is without doubt a luxury item. But it still fulfils a practical purpose, and if you like tennis, and have the space and the money to install a court of your own, then why not? To put one in such a location, however, is a pretty odd choice, similar to putting a garden shed right in front of the rear window of the lounge.

We go to all sorts of measures to try to hide things in gardens. One of the most common reactions is to use colour, either a dark, matt green or plain old black. Yet neither colour works well; both absorb a lot of light, which actually make the object you are trying to hide more rather than less visible. It's far better to either use no colour at all – allowing timber to gradually fade to silver grey for example – or use recessive paint finishes, especially light greys, which 'disappear' against the sky.

The other thing we do is to cover the unsightly object with something of exactly the same size and dimensions, so we cover an ugly building with a solid block of plants, which only serves to emphasise its shape. A more effective way to conceal an unpleasant object is to hide its outline, so rather than using solid blocks of planting to obscure an object, instead try using a mixture of vertically and horizontally shaped plants or structures to break up the outline. Alternatively, make a virtue out of an unattractive necessity. Bins can be hidden away in a neat little cabin with a green roof, whilst sheds can be clad with attractive materials and turned into a feature.

As for Anne and Geoff's tennis court, after much talk of building up levels to hide it, and sinking areas of the garden too, they eventually decided they could live without tennis and ripped it up to make a wildlife pond instead.

KEEP CALM AND CARRY ON

Wildflower meadows

OPPOSITE Wildflower meadows are vitally important habitats for a huge range of native species such as the common blue butterfly.

OPPOSITE The plans for Anne and Geoff's garden seek to blur the edges between the meadow and gardened areas by mixing formality and informality in the planting.

Amongst the plans for Ann and Geoff's garden is a wildflower meadow area, extending from near the house out into an existing paddock and then along the entire length and beyond the old flint curtilage wall. Really good wildflower meadows don't just happen by accident; they are actually a consequence of a number of factors coming together, usually over a long period of time – centuries sometimes. Agriculture is the reason for the existence of meadows, and the need to produce hay to provide winter feed for livestock. This ancient practice involves allowing areas of wild grass and flowers to grow uninterrupted until midsummer, when they were then cut and the grass left to dry for hay, which was then collected and stacked, in more recent years being baled using a machine. Once the meadow had greened up and recovered sufficiently from the cut, normally by autumn, sheep would be put on to graze until late winter. This combination of factors, and an absence of any chemical controls or fertilisers, ensured sweet hay for livestock but also a wildflower-rich meadow that wild animals such as butterflies, moths and small mammals could thrive in.

But old hay meadows are not especially productive, and the modern

practice of silage production, which involves using large amounts of fertiliser and chemicals to create copious growth of emerald green grass that can be harvested at least twice a year, has had a devastating effect on both the old meadows and the wildlife that once used to thrive alongside them.

It's Ann's childhood memories of walking through wildflower meadows in Northumberland that is in part responsible for her desire to have her own meadow in their new garden, along with her love of wildlife. It would seem like the easiest thing to do, but trying to re-create something with so many complex interactions isn't without

problems. Firstly, the soil needs to be 'unimproved'; the fertility of the soil reduced by stripping the topsoil away, exposing the less fertile subsoil. In a smaller garden this might be as simple as stripping off the turf and the top couple of inches of soil. Once this soil has been cultivated it can be sown, ideally using seed collected from a local source as this will contain plants that are genetically specific to the area, the optimum time for sowing being late autumn or, if that opportunity is missed, late winter. Once established, the meadow will need maintaining in a way that echoes the traditional cycles of hay harvesting and sheep grazing, with mechanical mowers taking the place of four-legged ovines!

'The beauty of native flowers and grasses, with butterflies flitting from bloom to bloom and small mammals and amphibians scurrying about among the foliage, is hard to beat'

Whilst trying to recreate a meadow isn't exactly straightforward, it is well worth the effort, even on a small scale. The beauty of native flowers and grasses, with butterflies flitting from bloom to bloom and small mammals and amphibians scurrying about among the foliage, is hard to beat; and, once established in the right setting, like Ann and Geoff's garden, it can look as if it has been there for centuries.

AN ENGLISHMAN'S HOME
IS HIS CASTLE

They say that an Englishman's home is his castle, but there can't be many of us who get to say that for real. Jason and Demetra Lindsay can, having inherited a large but rather crumbling Queen Anne house with various barns and outbuildings as well as a fairly unusual garden building – a huge Norman keep over 800 years old!

Jason Lindsay is descended from the founders of Hedingham Castle, continuing an occupation of this site by the family that has lasted for over 800 years. In recent years Hedingham, like many other stately homes in Britain, has suffered from the combined challenges of death duty taxes, gradual deterioration and a lack of people willing to work the land, and sadly now only a fragment of what was once a great estate now remains. The Lindsays moved in during 2005 with only portions of the house habitable, and have spent the intervening time trying to make it a home for their three young children, as well as working hard to make the estate pay for itself by turning it into a venue for weddings and events.

With so many drains on the estate's finances, and faced with pressing upkeep problems such as leaking roofs and damp in the walls, the garden has understandably taken a bit of a back seat. But the garden has its own fascinating history and is full of interesting features such as a dovecot, dating from 1720, as well as a brick Tudor bridge that at one point led to a Real Tennis court where, allegedly, Henry VIII once played. The most dominant feature in the garden is a large body of water known as the Long Shank, which frames magnificent views to and from house, the views embellished by venerable lime trees planted to the sides of the water.

ABOVE Jason and Demetra Lindsay have taken on the daunting task of restoring the gardens at Hedingham Castle, which has been in Jason's family for over 800 years.

But just as the house has suffered the ravages of time and circumstance, so has the garden. The drive to the house, which should show off the grandeur of the house to the visitor, is lined with hugely overgrown laurels and conifers, ruining the effect. And yet the bones of a wonderful garden are still there to find. The overgrown nature of the drive means many beautiful trees, such as a wonderful paper-bark maple (*Acer griseum*), are lost behind a lumpy vista of mundane shrubbery. Needing the garden to work just as hard as the house in order to pay its keep, Jason and Demetra have some tough decisions to make in tackling this overgrown, neglected garden.

ABOVE A new crinkle crankle beech hedge (1) ensures some privacy is restored to the driveway after the completed clearance of overgrown shrubs along it – a move triggered in part to help uncover a particularly beautiful paper bark maple (2). The newly opened vista (3) shows off the house to much better effect, whilst a mixture of wildflower and bulbs (4) lines the drive and contrasts with the tightly mown grass.

Hard landscaping in a neglected garden

OPPOSITE Such was the scale of work at Hedingham that heavy machinery (top left) was required to carry out a lot of it. Pre-existing features, such as the beautiful snowdrop walks (top right) were improved through the clearance of self-sown saplings, additional water features, including a restored informal pond next to the old dovecote (middle left), have been added, whilst the Norman keep (centre) is a dominant garden feature.

Taking on a neglected, overgrown garden can be a daunting challenge, whether a large historic garden like the one at Hedingham or a domestic back garden in any city, town or village. Just working out where on earth to start work can be a headache-inducing, overwhelming experience. As a consequence, overgrown gardens quite often stay overgrown for some time!

To tackle an overgrown garden most effectively, you first need to have a really good understanding of what is already there. Try to work out the original layout of the garden; check to see whether you can find any hard landscaping features like paths and seating areas lurking under the weeds and mess. Depending on how long the garden has been neglected these can be quite well hidden, so a little gentle excavation might be required. Sometimes the route of an overgrown path will be obvious due to yellowing of the grass or weeds that have grown over it, or unevenness compared with the surrounding ground. If you do uncover an old path, you might consider reinstating it, but the chances are that it will either be beyond repair or in the wrong place. In this case the materials could potentially be reused as the base for a new path or patio.

A good understanding of the layout and structure of a neglected garden can also help to highlight why a particular feature or plant is where it is. The presence of an unearthed patio in a seemingly random location might make complete sense once you observe the passage of the sun and realise that it is the sunniest spot in the garden, or the position of a bog planting in one corner might seem surprising until you realise it is where all the water in the garden runs to in times of heavy rain.

'Try to work out the original layout of the garden; check to see whether you can find any hard landscaping features like paths and seating areas lurking under the weeds and mess'

Before you do any kind of serious digging – i.e. deeper than 1m – check with local utility companies and get a plan of the underground utilities. The chances are they are far below the depth that you will ever dig to, but better safe than sorry. And be careful before you take a saw to a rickety fence or a sledge hammer to an old wall, because it may not actually be yours to demolish. Check the deeds of your house, or talk to your neighbours, before taking on a potentially costly and un-neighbourly project.

Working with existing planting

A little judicious 'editing' can work wonders in the garden, often just through the timely removal of a branch, or an individual plant. But working out where on earth to start – what to remove and which plant to take out first – can be extremely difficult, especially if the plants concerned are mature and of sizeable stature. As with hard landscaping features it pays to understand the layout and structure of the garden. Quite often, boundary trees will have been planted for a very particular reason, to help screen an unsightly building or structure. Removing, say, a mature shrub from a the garden boundary to free up space or improve light levels may seem like a good idea, until its gone and you are left with a view of the local meat-rendering plant…

Add to this the problem that, once you start taking out plants, it can be hard to stop. At Hedingham, Jason and Demetra decided to tackle the overgrown planting on the driveway up to the house to reveal the presence of the building, restore a sense of grandeur to the experience of arrival and to rescue some rather lovely plants that had become lost. They assessed the drive and selected a number of plants that they hoped would be worth keeping once the clearing was underway. However, what they quickly discovered was that once shrubs become overgrown they tend to become misshapen and can often be completely dead on one side. As a result, only a couple of the plants they had selected for keeping were worth saving, and what had been planned as a fairly modest restoration instead became a massive job. Though this situation might sound terrifying, it's worth remembering that sometimes it's better to start afresh with a new planting than carry on with an old, overgrown and potentially unsafe mess. With the right plants, decent soil preparation and aftercare, it will be only a matter of a couple of years before a replacement planting looks established.

Before going too far with removing established plants in your garden, there are also some practical and legal considerations that you must be aware of. Old or significant gardens often have listed status or might be included in a conservation area, AONB (area of outstanding natural beauty)

ABOVE The 'Long Shank' at Hedingham is an historically and visually important feature, with sweeping views from the house that have been adversely affected by later additions of planting such as the yew hedge across the main lawn, which interrupts the view.

or national park, in which case you will almost certainly need to apply to your local authority before any significant work takes place to get the advice of their tree and planning officers. Individual trees can sometimes be protected by tree protection orders and there can be quite hefty fines for interfering with such plants. You should also be aware of nesting animals that might be disturbed by felling and clearing – in the UK it is illegal to disturb a nest site. To avoid the latter, try to carry out any clearing work during autumn and winter, outside the nesting season.

ABOVE With an established garden it is important to carefully consider the existing features before taking action. Trees or shrubs might frame a particular view (left), or obscure an eyesore, whilst other plants may hide their charms for much of the year, but be incredibly beautiful when in flower such as this *Pieris* (right).

Thinking green

ABOVE You don't need a big garden or allotment to grow vegetables – the smallest of spaces, can be suitable for growing, as these 'reinvented' containers prove.

RIGHT If you have the space, giving over a couple of raised beds to growing food can help to reduce your carbon footprint, by reducing the need to buy imported vegetables. It's also great fun, highly educational and enables you to know exactly what has gone into making the food that you eat.

We live in a time when concern for the environment is a topic of conversation, driver for legislation and a source of often contradictory and conflicting advice from those who are supposed to be 'in the know'. Most of us would probably like to live in a manner that is less damaging to the planet, but with so many opposing views and contradictory so-called evidence it is hard to see how to do so. In recent years we have all become accustomed to the idea of recycling, and huge investment has gone in to improving recycling facilities and collection of waste, but instead of engendering a more responsible attitude to waste it has merely changed the way we dispose of rubbish – where once we would throw everything into a single bin and then absolve ourselves of any responsibility, we are now encouraged to put our rubbish into five bins instead, yet are still largely blissfully ignorant of what happens to it.

In the face of all of this our gardens, and the way we garden, seem rather inconsequential compared with the seemingly unstoppable challenges of climate change. But our gardens have a very positive role to play in connecting us with nature, wildlife and the wider environment, and in a modest but important way can help us to make a contribution toward reducing our impact on the planet.

Just as gardens have the capacity to be complete works of art, so gardening can be an expression of nature. To grow a plant from seed requires a basic understanding of the natural environment, an appreciation of simple science and a quality that is in increasingly short supply in our modern world – patience. And the resulting plants that grow from a seed sown from our own hand, whether to admire for their beauty or savour

OPPOSITE Planting
trees is a popular
way of offsetting
your carbon
footprint, but the
other benefits that
trees bring to the
landscape – filtering
out pollution,
providing homes for
animals and birds, as
well as making our
cities, towns and the
countryside more
pleasant places to be
– are all just as
important.

55

*Thought
Process*

for their taste, gives a satisfaction quite unlike anything else – not the
instance gratification of acquisition but an almost childlike excitement, a
sense of, 'I grew that!'

Gardens can also be the place where we can make a small contribution
toward the health of the planet, or at the very least enjoy ourselves in a way
that isn't detrimental to the environment. Plants help to reduce pollution
and produce oxygen, and can provide food for humans, which in turn helps
to reduce our carbon footprint because the less we need to buy from shops,
which in some cases will have been imported from abroad, the less we add
to transport pollution. And the ultimate destination for plants – the compost
heap or wormery – can be a veritable hub of virtuous activity, helping to
dramatically cut the amount of recyclable green waste that we throw away
be processing it and reusing it in the garden.

Encouraging wildlife

ABOVE Gardens provide a range of habitats for wildlife through the plants and features that comprise them. But installing bird feeders and habitat boxes, such as this ladybird box, can enhance the wildlife value further.

OPPOSITE Garden plants provide a feast for wildlife, be it in the form of fruit, nuts, seeds or pollen and nectar, essential for animals like the red admiral butterfly.

Aside from the benefits to the wider environment, our gardens can help to support the local wildlife that relies on domestic gardens for food and habitats. Gardens are like corridors for wildlife, linking our towns and cities with the wider countryside, allowing more mobile animals to pass from one to the other. They also form the vital green space in what might otherwise be an entirely built environment – the lungs of the city.

Garden plants can provide food for animals in the form of pollen and nectar which can feed a wide variety of insects including bees, butterflies and moths, and although non-native garden plants can't always provide the very specific food source required by the larval stages of insects (the orange tip butterfly caterpillar will only dine out on two or three native plants, including *Cardamine pratensis*), they can provide food for the adult insects over a longer period, as there are non-native garden plants that flower when native flowers are in short supply.

Trees are a wildlife habitat par excellence, with a mature oak tree providing a home for an estimated 20,000 individual creatures – from microscopic bugs to owls. Very few of us have room for an oak in our back garden, but even a small tree can be of significance to wildlife, especially one that produces fruit and nuts for food. If there is no room for a tree, then shrubs and hedgerows are ideal nesting places for birds, insects and small mammals – and if there isn't much room for them there are nest boxes that can be bought or made to do the same job.

A garden that is friendly for wildlife also tends to be a healthy garden, as without excessive intervention in the form of chemical controls a natural balance can build up, so that the 'pest' insects that nibble plants will be nibbled themselves by predatory animals. There will undoubtedly come a time when some type of intervention is required, but if this is kept to a minimum it gives the garden and nature the chance to look after things first, rather than trying to heal the damage inflicted by impatience. There is so much more joy to be had from a garden that is full of colourful flowers and colourful wildlife, rather than a sterile environment, and if children are using the garden they will adore the adventure they embark on every time they venture out.

LIVING THE GOOD LIFE DOWN IN THE VALLEY

ABOVE Trevor and Sarah Woods have given up an urban life to try to lead more sustainable lifestyles with their three children in the heart of the Welsh countryside. The plot of land and house they have bought is largely derelict, and their budget is very tight – so they'll need to be creative and recycle or reinvent materials to get what they want.

Sarah and Trevor Woods gave up their urban lives in a spa town to pursue the goal of a near-self-sufficient, environmentally aware lifestyle in the countryside. Having sold up their property, they were able to buy a dilapidated, near-derelict farmhouse and five acres of pasture in rural Wales. Their dream is restore the house as a home for themselves and their three young children, and turn the garden into an outdoor space for the whole family to use for fun, entertaining and relaxing, whilst turning the bulk of the land over to the production of food.

In order to realise their dream for the garden, however, Sarah and Trevor have a huge hurdle to overcome – they have almost no budget with which to achieve their aims. Instead they are relying on the generous help of a garden designer friend to give them the guidance they need, allied with a mixture of bartering for products, online trawling for bargains, skip diving (utilising the materials found in skips generated by building projects and domestic waste disposal) and recycling or reinventing the objects they find on site. And whilst they do all this they are enduring their second cold winter in a cramped caravan, which the whole family share with five rescue dogs of varying 'vintages' and sizes.

Sarah and Trevor's garden is located in one of the most beautiful parts of mid-Wales, about 30 miles from the Irish Sea and in a valley surrounded by hills that range from gently rolling to steep-sided, eventually giving way to mountain ranges. It's a beautiful location to live and garden in, complete with a small river that runs through the site and forms one of the boundaries of the property. But gardening here isn't without challenges. The climate can be tough, freezing in winter and exposed to winds. And whilst the rain in Wales may be a cliché, there is no doubt it is true here – the rainfall average is over 1200mm per annum, three times as much as parts of the south-east of England.

So, with climatic challenges, a minute budget and high aspirations, how can Sarah and Trevor make their ambitious plans work?

ABOVE The near-derelict farmhouse forms the fulcrum of the site, and when rebuilding is completed the new garden will radiate from it. The new design integrates an existing green roofed barn that Sarah and Trevor built when they first bought the plot (1). Currently used as storage for most of their possessions, this is set to become the chicken shed. The new fruit and vegetable garden will be created on the site of the existing kitchen garden (2) but will utilise raised beds to improve growing conditions.

To help create their new garden, Sarah and Trevor have been able to draw upon the expertise of designer Jill Fenwick. Jill has created a plan for a new family garden in the area adjacent to the house, which includes an outdoor living space complete with a fire pit to help keep cold evenings at bay (3) as well as an outdoor dining area to enable the family to enjoy al fresco dining (4). An unusual water feature and a variety of structural planting to soften the hard landscaping and architecture of the house complete the plan.

Growing your own

OPPOSITE Sarah and Trevor's sustainable dreams began with the purchase of a near-derelict farmhouse. Growing at least a proportion of their own fruit and vegetables is a key part of their aims, which they hope to achieve by creating a kitchen garden and orchard, whilst livestock also form an important part of the Wood's sufficiency plans.

Trevor and Sarah are determined to make their land work for them by producing as much food as possible for the family, and also providing grazing and living space for the rescue battery hens and Cancun pigs that patrol the pasture. 'Growing your own' has undergone a renaissance in recent years and it's easy to see why – there is something incredibly satisfying about growing your own food.

Taking a tiny seed, sowing it and watching it grow into something that can feed you, your friends and family, and knowing everything that has happened to that crop during its growth, is both rewarding and reassuring. It's also something that everyone can engage in, and is a great way of introducing children to the idea of plants, as well as being an easy way to keep fit. Best of all, you don't need a big plot of the type that Trevor and Sarah have available to do it. A container or two, or a window box, can be enough to grow a range of vegetables, herbs and salad crops, even potatoes.

Trevor and Sarah may have a lot of space in which to grow but that doesn't mean their ambitions are problem free. For one thing, the cold and often wet weather in their area can mean that the growing season is much shorter than in warmer areas. Early in the season the soil can be too wet and heavy to cultivate, making it impossible to sow seeds into. And it can take much longer for the soil to warm up sufficiently, further delaying sowing. Damp and cool conditions also suit particular pests, especially slugs and snails, which can devastate vegetable crops, especially brassicas such as cabbages. There are also a host of fungal diseases that thrive in warm, damp and close conditions once summer arrives and the temperatures rise.

The best way to keep soil in top condition in wet areas is by using raised beds. Often made from timber, either purpose made or hand built, but also available made from a range of materials including recycled plastic, raised beds ensure the growing medium is raised out of the worst of the wet. In effect, they are like oversized boxes full of soil. Because the sides of the raised beds are exposed to the sun, the soil within the bed warms up earlier in the season, drains more readily and can therefore be sown into much earlier. Metal or plastic hoops can be fitted to the beds and covered with clear plastic to create a warmer growing environment, rather like a greenhouse, and once crops are established the plastic can be replaced with a protective mesh that can help to keep pests at bay.

Reinvention in the garden

As Plato once observed, and Trevor and Sarah have discovered over the course of their garden project, necessity is the mother of invention. When you have almost no budget with which to make a garden, reusing, reinventing and recycling objects and materials to give them a new life is a priority. Fortunately there are plenty of opportunities to reuse items in the garden that might otherwise just be thrown away, in doing so giving them a new lease of life and reducing waste to landfill. Gardeners have been good at this for centuries; reusing scraps of baler twine or old bits of wood to tie up runner beans or fill the gaps in a fence, for example.

Scrap materials can be used in a number of ways in the garden, especially as containers for plants. A galvanised water tank or old section of air conditioning duct can make a stylish planting container that will have the look of an expensive purchase but cost almost nothing. A length of iron or plastic guttering, planted with low-growing house leeks (*Sempervivum* species and cultivars) can make an architecturally interesting living sculpture, as can an old copper or steel cooking pan. Even old sanitary ware – toilets, sinks and the like – can be turned into planters, although you will need to decide for yourself at what point curio becomes bad taste!

To find all these interesting materials, you need to be willing to look in the right places. This can mean an online trawl, a visit to a local scrap metal merchant or architectural salvage, or a bit of peering into builders skips. There are also bargains to be had in the form of purpose-made equipment that other people no longer need. Trevor and Sarah managed to get hold of a solar dome – a type of large glasshouse made as a geodesic dome – for next to nothing as it was no longer wanted and would have cost the owner money to dispose of. They've also used the slate innards from an old billiard table to make a beautiful outdoor dining table, something that (even in a country as rich in slate as Wales) would cost a fortune. Regular checks on recycling websites will often throw up similar bargains.

'There are plenty of opportunities to reuse items in the garden that might otherwise just be thrown away'

ABOVE Giving new life to objects and materials that have already served a purpose, rather than throwing them away, is increasingly important as the waste we produce mounts up. A salvage sculpture can make an interesting curio in the garden – even if it's just for the sake of irony!

LEFT Collecting builders' waste for reuse can offer up all sorts of interesting opportunities for reinvention. Waste pipes can become planting containers, offcuts of timber or stone reused, while paving and walling can be lifted, brushed up and re-laid.

BELOW A little time spent on recycling websites can throw up all sorts of great bargains. Sarah and Trevor found this geodesic dome online, inside which they now grow frost-tender veggies such as cucumbers and peppers for the garden.

CONSERVATION ON THE CLIFF TOP

ABOVE The island landscape of Guernsey is dramatic and beautiful, but like many small islands there are pressures on the environment that pose significant challenges.

Of all the places to make a garden, on top of a cliff in the middle of the English Channel must be one of the most interesting and challenging. Vanessa and Ed Adams bought their modest bungalow not for the property so much as for the spectacular vistas. Four acres of cliff top on the south-western tip of the Channel Island of Guernsey overlook a beautifully craggy bay with just a few other properties to spoil the illusion that it might just be an uninhabited island.

Vanessa and Ed see the development of their garden as a chance to create something that is in tune with the local environment, whilst at the same time being a viable family space for themselves and their two young sons. It's a pretty big challenge: the site is overgrown with bracken and brambles, with a few remaining shrubs and trees planted years before – the ghostly remnants of a previous garden. The site also slopes rapidly away from the house down to the cliff path, below which is an almost sheer drop of thirty metres or so to the sea.

The rock that forms the island of Guernsey is granite, one of the toughest of all rocks. Above this the soil on the island 'floats', held down largely by the plants that grow on it. This makes removing weeds something of a double-edged sword – it is important that they do so to enable areas to be cleared and replanted, but at the same time there is a very real risk that, if left for too long, the topsoil will simply blow away in the prevailing sea winds.

Vanessa and Ed must also face the tensions that will arise as a result of trying to create something that is ecologically sensitive but at the same time a viable garden. They want to include practical features in their garden such as play areas for their boys, an outdoor dining area, as well as somewhere to grow fruit and vegetables. But flat space is in very short supply in the steeply sloping site, and the obvious solution to this – putting in a series of terraces using materials like stone or timber – is time-consuming and expensive.

There's no doubting Vanessa and Ed's commitment to preserving and improving their local environment, but how much can their garden be expected to achieve? Intelligent design will be needed to ensure they don't end up with a space that is neither garden nor wild habitat, that meets neither their needs nor their dreams, and that, far from being a shining example of a new way of gardening in tune with nature, might just be a bit of a mess.

ABOVE The area (1) behind the house has been levelled to make a flat play area for Vanessa and Ed's boys to enjoy. On this steeply sloping site flatter areas have been created by terracing, using dry stone walling and railway sleeper timbers (2). A winding path (3) provides a journey through the garden whilst following the contours of the slope, making for a safer, less precipitous route. Timber jetties (4) form the turns in the path, and provide areas to sit and enjoy the spectacular views.

Nurture or nature

OPPOSITE One of the big difficulties, when gardening with nature, is that the aesthetic tipping point between attractively wild and unkempt and mess can be extremely fine. Railway sleeper sets smothered in wildflowers bring together the deliberately planned features of a garden with the randomness of wild beauty.

Gardening is, by definition, the manipulation and subjugation of nature. Or perhaps more accurately the attempted manipulation and control of nature, because nature will always, without question, win out. Even if a garden is only left untended for a matter of days or weeks, the first signs of re-colonisation by nature will appear in the form of a covering of weeds. Left for longer, grasses, brambles and eventually trees will take over from manicured borders – it's the way of nature, and always has been.

The tension between where a garden ends and nature takes over is especially difficult in places where the landscape is under threat, or is of particular ecological sensitivity. Vanessa and Ed Adams' garden in Guernsey is representative of the challenges and sometimes seemingly imponderable questions that face anyone wanting to garden in an environmentally sensitive way. Guernsey wrestles with all the same environmental issues as the rest of the Britain: overcrowding, pollution, waste disposal and so on. But on a small island of just 24 square miles, and with a population of 60,000 (that's 2,500 people per square mile) the problems are amplified. Vanessa and Ed want to respond to these challenges by sensitively managing their bit of cliff top, partly simply for their own enjoyment but also for loftier ambitions, to offer a possible template by which other cliff-top gardens in Guernsey might grow.

The difficulty for anyone wanting to garden with nature is that it's impossible to decide how much of it to allow in, and how much to control and keep out. Whilst we might like to think we are in control of nature, we clearly aren't. Therefore, how can a garden be created without accepting that intervention will have to be made, and that in some instances it might not always be beneficial to nature in every sense?

The answer, to an extent at least, is that it can't. The manipulation required to make a garden will inevitably cause disruption to the natural state of things – from disturbing the soil flora through digging, to removing a tree or a shrub that may have been a nesting site for birds. But the reality is that nature itself can be far more destructive: creating forest fires, blowing up hurricanes and whipping the sea into tsunami. And at the end of the disruption caused by making a garden, the result is something at worst benign, perhaps beneficial, that will provide habitats and food for all sorts of animals, as well as pleasure for humans too.

'Even if a garden is only left untended for a matter of days or weeks, the first signs of re-colonisation by nature will appear'

By the seaside

Gardening by the sea throws up a range of specific challenges that aren't faced by gardeners anywhere else. Sea winds are laden with salt, which can scorch and burn foliage, cause plants to wilt and in the most extreme cases completely defoliate. The strength and persistence of the winds can cause plants to become stunted, one-sided versions of what they should really be, turning big forest trees into bonsai. As they can bent over, broken or even pulled from the ground, and the soil around them blown away into the sky, it can be a challenge to get new plants to establish in such persistently windy conditions. The bright sunlight that comes with a seaside location can cause wilting and limit the range of plants that can be successfully used, as well as washing out soft, pastel colours that would work well elsewhere.

But gardening by the sea isn't all bad news. The high light levels and wide horizons create a purity of light usually found in places like the Mediterranean fringe. Strong, bright colours look beautiful by the seaside and colours that would usually look too bold or overbearing can be used with enthusiasm. Likewise, found materials such as driftwood, beach pebbles and the detritus of the seaside can look terribly kitsch in an inland garden, but look perfectly lovely in their natural environment.

And then there are the plants. Nature has provided a great bounty of those that can tolerate seaside living, as well as a number specialist plants that absolutely have to be by the seaside to thrive. Some, such as sea holly (*Eryngium maritimum*) send down deep, thick, questing tap roots that carry out several functions; acting as a storage vessel for starch and sap, collecting whatever water lurks far down in the ground, and anchoring the plant firmly to terra firma – no mean feat when you might be submerged by the tides or whipped by onshore winds. On the California coast there is a little plant called *sand verbena*, which is quite uncommon, and which has sticky leaves and flowers that cause sand to be 'glued' to the plant, which helps to act as a protective shield from the harsh environment.

Understanding the challenges and responding to them sympathetically, rather than trying to fight against them, is the key to creating a successful seaside garden.

ABOVE A seaside location need not preclude having a garden, but it does require a lot more thought and planning to ensure the correct plants and practices are being followed.

BELOW In Vanessa and Ed's garden, only those plants that are adapted to the particular seaside conditions, such as *Elymus magellanicus* (centre), native ferns (centre right) and the shoreline-growing sea holly *Eryngium maritimum* (bottom right) will thrive. Seating areas (bottom left) are fitted with timber screens to provide shelter from the wind for those enjoying the superb sea views.

VISION

2

'God is in the details'
Ludwig Mies van der Rohe

You don't have to be a genius to make a garden, but great gardens often feel like the work of genius, effortlessly combining a mixture of art, craft and graft to create a living and changing three-dimensional space. Almost 300 years ago, Alexander Pope adopted *genius loci* (genius of the place) as a central principle of landscape design. His mantra of respecting the individual qualities of a place, developing an understanding of nature and applying that knowledge foremost when designing a garden is still as valid as ever:

Consult the genius of the place in all;
That tells the waters or to rise, or fall;
Or helps th'ambitious hill the heav'ns to scale,
Or scoops in circling theatres the vale;
Calls in the country, catches opening glades,
Joins willing woods, and varies shades from shades,
Now breaks, or now directs, th'intending lines;
Paints as you plant, and, as you work, designs.
Epistle IV, to Richard Boyle, Earl of Burlington

Today we are exposed to design in a variety of guises – from industrial to architectural, automotive to technological. The aftermath of the Second World War created both the opportunity and the market for well-designed, often minimalist products – with everything from pottery, glassware and furniture to electronics, automobiles and architecture becoming the subject of fresh thinking and uncluttered design. Just as with Pope's *genius loci*, the philosophies of the designers behind these products have also influenced us. Amongst these are the ten design commandments of Dieter Rams, the German industrial designer most associated with the groundbreaking Braun products of the 1950s and 60s:

1. *Good design is innovative.*
2. *Good design makes a product useful.*
3. *Good design is aesthetic.*
4. *Good design helps us to understand a product.*
5. *Good design is unobtrusive.*
6. *Good design is honest.*
7. *Good design is durable.*
8. *Good design is consequent to the last detail.*
9. *Good design is concerned with the environment.*
10. *Good design is as little design as possible.*

Rams' principles can be applied to any discipline, even garden design. We want our gardens to be useful, but also aesthetically pleasing. Durability is certainly important, as is a concern for the environment. But what really makes a well-designed garden is a considered combination of the various components (and not just the practical ones such as the shed or the washing line) that go together to form the whole.

If consideration is given to the details such as how space is organised and divided, as well as to the effects that certain important elements such as light, colour and texture have on that space, then your garden can be transformed. This vision process, informed by the practicalities covered within 'Thought Process' will help you to create a template for the design of your garden. It is also the best opportunity throughout the course of the whole process to have some fun and really allow your imagination to run free. Professional designers love to push against the boundaries of a brief, dreaming up all sorts of unusual solutions to the issues posed by its most practical aspects, and this is a great chance for you to do the same.

Space

OPPOSITE Tiny spaces can be incredibly challenging to design– they can easily look overly contrived or be so crammed with 'stuff' that they become unusable. Here a small space is maximised by using vertical and horizontal planting to blur the area's narrow boundaries, whilst a table and chairs act as a focal point to draw the eye from the walls to the centre of the space.

RIGHT Spatial division in the garden isn't just about making room for the things you need; it's a fundamental principle of the aesthetics of design. Even a simple area of lawn can become its own space when viewed through a screen of surrounding plants.

Whether commuting to work on overly busy, traffic-filled roads or shopping in the local supermarket with its jammed isles and interminable snaking queues of shoppers, all of us wish we had a little more space from time to time. We need to feel like free people, rather than caged animals. And yet, as a consequence of modern living, we are constantly battling against an overall lack of space – whether that be a dearth of practical storage space in our homes or just a little elbow room on the train. The space 'poverty' that we suffer from affects every aspect of our lives and results in us valuing what little space that we do have ever more highly.

Our gardens offer us a chance to experience a comparative rarity, the simple, unalloyed joy of free outdoor space. But even here this precious taste of space is squeezed, our homes are now often built closer and closer together and our gardens are crammed into ever-shrinking plots. The proximity of other houses often means our gardens are overlooked, with the fences and hedges of neighbouring gardens becoming intrusive, overbearing structures as we struggle to control what little privacy we have left. And though our gardens may be smaller, our desire for space is not reduced. In these circumstances the need to apply considered and thoughtful design to the garden becomes even more important if the little space that is available is to be used to best effect, with all our practical considerations taken care of in a way that doesn't just meet our needs, but allows, in this ever-more pressurised world, for a few dreams to be dreamed and escapes to be made.

Divisions of space

OPPOSITE Spatial division can be as simple as the allocation of a place for a particular feature, such as an outdoor dining table and chairs or a garden pond; or can be far more considered and precise in execution, using a series of dividing features to create garden rooms that have their own distinct character.

Most gardens are, in effect, boxes. They may vary in shape and size but the majority will typically have four boundaries – these could be fences, walls, hedges, other properties, or a combination thereof.

The natural reaction to the urge to maximise the space within these boundaries is to make the middle of the box as empty and clutter-free as possible: emptiness equals space. So flower borders and trees are pushed out to the edges of the garden and it ends up looking rather like the drum of a washing machine after a wash, with everything flung out to the sides and a gaping hole in the middle. And yet having nothing but space can actually make the garden appear *smaller*; with the boundaries clearly visible, our minds are able to read the space for what it is.

But, if you apply a little trickery and instead try to divide up the box within the boundaries you can deceive your eyes into believing the space is bigger than it actually is. Creating particular areas or 'rooms' within the garden that have a different atmosphere – either through planting, hard landscaping or something as simple as the quality of light – can create a sense of moving through an experience, rather than viewing something from a distance as a detached observer; because what our eyes cannot see is always more intriguing and alluring than what they can.

LEFT This precipitous garden has been deftly divided into a series of mini garden rooms, created by forming the garden into three level areas by means of terraces, each with a distinct aesthetic flavour and strong architectural planting in the form of clipped box.

RIGHT Applying flowing, curving lines within the boundaries of a rectangular outline can help to break down the 'washing machine' effect, where planting is pushed to the outer boundaries of the garden, leaving a dull void in the middle.

'If you apply a little
trickery and divide
up the box within the
boundaries, you can
deceive your eyes
into believing the
space is bigger than
it actually is'

ABOVE Using a
variety of hard
materials including
timber decking and
stone paving, divided
by generous planting
areas, helps to create
the sensation of a
variety of different
spaces without the
need for vertical
barriers.

Vistas and focal points

OPPOSITE One of the ways that Clive and Debbie Morris intend to give their garden dramatic visual impact is through the intelligent use of focal points. This wire urn from Saling Hall in Essex sits amongst the frothy flowers of native cow parsley, which effectively complement the urn's colour and lightness of frame.

Our eyes are wonderful things, miracles of design with extraordinary power. But they do tend to wander. Even when seemingly fixed on one spot, they are constantly moving, re focussing and taking in new information. And yet, when there is something interesting or different to see, something that grabs our attention, our roving eyes pause, even if just for a moment.

The power of the well-placed 'eye catcher', as focal points are often called, has long been understood by landscape and garden designers. Many of the great gardens that were created between the late 17th and 19th centuries were designed with follies, temples, bridges and grottoes as focal points, often reinforced by strategically placed avenues of trees that would create narrow views or 'vistas' to lead the eye in their direction.

In the domestic garden, vistas and focal points can be effectively used to do one of two things: to either show something off, or to draw attention away from something that you would rather not make a point of. Though the space available in most gardens is likely to prevent the construction of a hermit's grotto or an elaborate mausoleum at the end of the garden path, a focal point can be almost anything that catches the

> '**A focal point can be almost anything that catches the eye – a piece of garden furniture, a brightly painted plant pot, even the shed**'

eye – a piece of garden furniture, a brightly painted plant pot, even the shed. In fact, the focal point doesn't even need to be in the garden, as borrowing interesting features from the landscape beyond will instantly help to make your space seem bigger and more interesting.

But whatever the nature of the focal point, the vital rule to follow is that it is deliberately and consciously framed. There's no point in having half a dozen brightly painted pots dotted around in open space hoping they will act as focal points; that wandering eye will simply read them as a gaggle of lurid pots. And this is where the vista comes in. A grand garden might have sweeping alleys of majestic trees to frame a view, but in a smaller garden a simple vista can be created by making an aperture in a hedge, or arranging a group of pots in such a way that it frames an interesting feature.

By establishing multiple focal points framed from different view points throughout the garden you can really begin to exploit the space, creating numerous points of interest. Even the smallest garden will benefit from a carefully placed focal point. Surprisingly perhaps, even though they will be intimately known to you, these focal points will continue to catch your eye.

LEFT The borrowed view is one of the great classical landscape gardening motifs, but usually in reference to borrowing the view of distant fields, lakes or valleys. Here, on a more modest scale, a pierced brick wall offers views beyond one part of the garden to another with a different planting style. The principle of the borrowed view still applies today, even in a small garden, and can apply to a carefully framed external view or to something within the garden that is deliberately picked out, as here.

Case Study *Sussex*

LEFT In Anne and Geoff's Sussex garden, one of the few remaining features – a faux classical sculpture of a woman – is being recycled into the new garden to continue its role as a focal point, watching over the view to the South Downs.

'By establishing multiple focal points framed from different view points throughout the garden you can really begin to exploit the space, creating numerous points of interest'

ABOVE Vistas are typically associated with gardens of scale, as here at Saling Hall in Essex where a classical, colonnaded building acts as the focal point to a long vista comprised of parallel plantings of shrubs, hedging and trees. But vistas need not be so grand; the combination of deliberately aligned features with a terminal point can be achieved on a much smaller scale. It's the composition that counts, not the size.

Taking a journey

One of the biggest weaknesses of the 'washing machine' garden, where there is nothing but an open space in the centre and a few borders flung out to the boundaries at the sides, is that there is no sense of being able to take a journey through the garden. When everything is on display, there is little or no imperative to step out into the garden and wander around the space, because you can see all too clearly that there is nothing to explore.

And yet, what makes a garden really interesting is combining the deliberately shown off – the focal points designed to draw your eye and the vistas used to frame them – with the concealed, the controlled, the just out of reach or round the corner. In this respect, the alignment and orientation of the humble garden path can play an important role in setting up the sense of a journey waiting to be taken, a little tease to make you want to venture off in search of where it might take you. A curving path automatically encourages the viewer to want to see around the corner, whilst a straight path with right-angle turns can lead the eye in stages through the garden, setting up multiple opportunities for 'events' to take place.

These 'events' can take many forms but each is in essence designed to act as natural punctuation in your journey around the garden. An event might be a focal point such as a bench which, when you reach it, beckons you to sit. If you're really clever, these events will open up the unexpected: sitting upon that bench, for example, could reveal another focal point in the opposite direction, whilst on walking through an archway you might be greeted with an unexpected change in planting style or a previously hidden open space or seating area.

RIGHT In a small garden the space for a journey will always be limited. But a journey can be taken with the eyes, from a static position, as much as on two feet. Here a number of factors combine to create the sense of a visual journey: the terminal focal point of a water feature flanked by *Cordyline*, the inset lawn surrounded by sleek stone paving, and two benches that invite use.

LEFT A mown grass path through a mini meadow of long grass and wildflowers creates a romantic, bucolic journey, the equal of anything that can be created with big budgets and hard landscaping. At Hedingham Castle the cessation of mowing in large parts of the garden has allowed wildflowers to become re-established and meadow walks to be created.

'What makes a garden really interesting is combining the deliberately shown off ...with the concealed, the controlled, the just out of reach or round the corner'

Vertical space

OPPOSITE Planted alongside a boundary barrier, pleached hornbeam avenues (top) help soften a garden's edges. Features such as pergolas (bottom right) or archways add vertical interest to a garden and serve a practical purpose as plant supports without occupying too much horizontal space, while a stepped series of planters against a wall (bottom left) can be a very effective way of getting both height into a garden and utilising an otherwise 'dead' space.

Given that we humans move through three dimensions, it's interesting that, when it comes to conceptualising our garden space, we tend to take a very two-dimensional approach. Whilst our gardens are measured in linear fashion (80ft x 20ft) or by square footage or metres, the vertical plane remains the great, unexplored frontier – a by-and-large limitless space that we tend to ignore. In part this is a result of our widely held (incorrect) belief that an empty void in the middle of the garden is the best way to maximise our garden space and that any tall features will compromise this. Perhaps there is also a fear of using features or plants with height in case they look out of scale, or cast unwanted shade where we want the maximum possible sun to enjoy.

However, far from shrinking the garden, exploring the vertical plane can help to make it seem much bigger. Vertical features draw the eye upwards and outward, and help to give your garden an interesting extra dimension. These features don't need to be massively tall – plants such as the common foxglove or hollyhock can draw the eye upwards even though neither is taller than 1.8m. Vertical structures can also play multiple roles in the garden; a pergola or archway can provide a vertical accent whilst also acting as a support for growing plants, a means of casting dappled shade and a mechanism for framing a vista or as a focal point; whilst obelisks – if carefully placed and used a recurring feature – can create a sense of rhythmic repetition. Whatever feature you chose, remember that the trick is not to confine it to the peripheries of your space. Instead try using it in the heart of the garden, so that rather than emphasising the smallness of a space it can balance it out, whilst adding drama and scale at the same time.

Five plants to add height

Echium pininana
A huge narrow spire smothered in blue flowers that are loved by bees.
2–4m x 90cm

Molinia 'Skyracer'
Fine, airy stems with a translucent quality and lovely golden autumn hues.
2m x 40cm

Eremurus robustus
Produces an impressive tall spike of pale pink flowers in June.
2m x 1.2m

Digitalis parviflora
Has very narrow spires of rusty brown flowers that are handsome en masse.
1.2m x 30cm

Juniperus scopulorum 'Skyrocket'
An evergreen conifer with a pencil-thin habit. A great vertical structure plant.
3m x 50cm

LEFT Bringing vertical features into the centre of the garden can seem counter-intuitive; our instinct is to push height to the boundaries and preserve the centre of the garden as open space. But as this mini avenue of pleached hornbeam demonstrates, adding vertical interest to the heart of the garden can add to the space in the garden rather than compromise it.

Scale, proportion and balance

Getting scale, proportion and therefore balance right in a garden can be a tricky exercise, especially when space is at a premium. In a small garden the need to fit in all the practical features required, along with a diversity of desirable elements, can lead to the overall effect being bitty or twee. When the features that form the boundaries or outlook of the garden are substantial, it can be even harder to keep things in scale – if your tiny plot is surrounded by towering buildings or looks out onto vast open fields, what then?

One way to help achieve a sense of balanced scale and proportion is to use the proportions of the house to set out the garden by making a scale drawing of the facade of the house and laying it over a drawing of the garden – a technique popularised by the groundbreaking British designer John Brookes. By doing so, the major features of the house begin to help determine where features in the garden begin and end in a very natural way. This doesn't work in every instance of course, but it's a useful tool in situations where the proportions of house and garden allow.

There are other simple guidelines that can help you to get the balance right. When setting out the dimensions of a planted border, ensuring that for every linear metre the border is half as wide again will help to prevent the creation of thin, 'mean' borders. Though there is a limit to how far this rule works, depending on the overall space of the garden, it is a helpful guide.

RIGHT Achieving the right scale and proportion in a really tiny garden can be a challenge. This very small courtyard garden features a dominant lead tank water feature and ornamental trellis surround painted the same colour. Although seemingly outsized at first glance, the scale of the water feature works – just because it is so bold.

LEFT Perspective affects scale and proportion as surely as actual physical size, and this can be manipulated to create different visual effects in the garden; creating a falsely elongated vista or foreshortening a view. Here the size of the summerhouse, the length of the path and the height of the hedges in the foreground are all in balance.

In a really tiny garden it can sometimes help to be deliberately bold with scale, upsizing pots, furniture and plants to create the illusion that the garden is larger, which works well providing some restraint is applied – too many massive pots and huge plants can leave you feeling Lilliputian. But it is certainly better than going the other way and filling a tiny space with tiny things, as this is guaranteed to make the space look very small indeed, and probably rather silly. It can also lead to a loss of cohesion as a clutter of tiny features, all jostling with one another for visual attention, is unlikely to make for a happy blend of elements.

There are instances of course when it helps to play with scale and proportion. Using a slightly undersized focal point, say a bench or garden building at the end of a vista, will make the object appear further away and the vista longer, in turn making the garden feel bigger. Vista lengths can also be cheated by accentuating perspective – gradually narrowing a path, or bringing the two sides of an avenue gradually closer together, will lengthen a view. Bear in mind though, that this technique does need to be carefully executed, as too sudden or dramatic a narrowing will appear too obvious a 'cheat'. Ultimately, the only foolproof way to ensure that the balance and proportion of features in the garden is right is to plan thoroughly, try them out on the ground, and be prepared to change them, if need be, as you put your plan into action.

ABOVE To avoid the visual confusion and general sense of incoherence that can be created in a small space when too great a variation of plants and hard landscaping materials are used, this small courtyard garden has been very simply planted using a restrained palette. The seating area uses paving stones that match the colour and materials of the house walls, with the result that the space appears larger than it actually is. The simplicity of the predominantly green planting, and the textural and repetitive qualities of the clipped box orbs all contribute to creating a calming, cohesive space; whilst the row of mature grape vines gives a sense of enclosure, of looking through plants, without impeding views or shrinking the available space.

ABOVE This small, shaded, courtyard city garden has been designed to make the most of the available space. A pair of large clipped bay trees, planted in containers, flank the entrance to a timber decked seating area, framing the view and delineating the end of one space – an area of stone paving and plants in terracotta pots – and marking out the beginning of another. Creating a focal point between the bay trees, a large clump of African lilies (*Zantedeschia aethiopica*) and slightly offset table and chairs invite the viewer into the seating area. The vertical space in this garden is well used too, with height from the boundary wall topped with trellis and the generous tree and shrub planting at the end of the courtyard.

Light

OPPOSITE The effect of light and shade can be as visually arresting as any flower or foliage combination in the garden. Here an ancient lantern in an alcove and the hatched shadow cast by a pierced timber screen, playing out against a plain, whitewashed wall, are all that is needed to create a beautiful composition.

Light is as fundamental to our existence and that of the majority of animal and plant species on Earth as oxygen. In more prosaic terms, light is vital for our wellbeing, and is a central component of the garden experience.

The amount of natural light that we have in our gardens depends on four factors: orientation, season, surroundings and content. Orientation is the direction a garden faces according to the compass and has a fundamental effect on natural light levels and light quality. As the principal source of natural light is the sun, orientation also influences how warm the garden gets, how quickly it cools off, whether the soil warms early in the growing season and so on. In simplistic terms, in the northern hemisphere a south-facing garden is sunny and warm, a north-facing garden shaded and cool, an east-facing garden sunny in the morning and warm for a few hours before cooling off, whilst a west-facing garden is sunny and warm during the afternoon and evening. There is no right or wrong to the orientation of a garden, just different conditions to understand and work with.

Light levels also vary according to the season, due to the relative position of the sun in our sky. During high summer the trajectory of the sun is at its most elevated, ensuring the maximum amount of light in open, south-facing gardens and the greatest amount of reflected light experienced in otherwise shaded north-facing gardens. By midwinter the sun is at its lowest, and even on a bright day the shadows cast by fences, trees and walls will last all day.

Surroundings can have a dramatic impact on light levels too. An open boundary, or one marked by a permeable barrier such as a chain link fence, will allow light through without casting a shadow, whilst a solid barrier like a timber fence or brick wall will either act as a sun and light trap, with the light and heat being reflected back from it, or will cast shade.

The content of the garden has rather more subtle implications for the intensity, quality and duration of light, as features of any description with verticality — be they shrubs, pots or posts — will cast shade. How deep that shade is will depend on the nature of the object casting it: a tree with a light canopy like silver birch (*Betula* species) casts a pleasant, dappled shade, whilst an evergreen conifer with dense foliage such as the popular hedge plant, yew (*Taxus baccata*), can cast shade as dense as that of a brick wall. The materials employed can also create interesting effects; light-reflective paint surfaces, water, light-coloured stone, and the nature of the plants — from the feathery plumes of an ornamental grass to the glossy leaf of a *Camellia* — will all change the way light is reflected, amplified or subdued.

Playing with natural light

OPPOSITE Very few shaded gardens are completely in shade all day. Here an understanding of where light and shade are cast has influenced the placement of a table and chairs, which sit in a pool of diffused light. The white-painted wall helps to reflect as much light as possible back into the garden.

The interplay of light and shade in a garden is what helps to bring it to life. It also offers us a range of opportunities to exploit; a naturally occurring pool of light can be the perfect spot for an eye-catching feature, lighting it up like a leading actor in a theatre spotlight, whilst complex shadows cast against reflective white paint can be as beautiful to look at as a planted border, the simplicity of the constantly changing shadows creating movement and shifts in mood throughout the course of the day.

Certain plants, such as ornamental grasses, have the ability to seemingly 'catch' light in their flowers or seed heads, whilst the capacity to create intricate patterns of light and shade is one of the key features of certain large-leaved, architectural plants. Through its ability to enhance light and reflect the sky and its surroundings, a body of water can also transform a garden space.

'A naturally occurring pool of light can be the perfect spot for an eye-catching feature, lighting it up like a leading actor in a theatre spotlight'

A gloomy side return, one of the most common of all urban garden experiences, can be turned from a space to be passed through in a hurry to something you will want to show off through the application of bright, light-reflective paint, light-coloured paving materials (which will reflect far more light than a matt, dark-coloured slate), containers and the planting of big, bold, glossy-leaved plants − many of which are big and bold precisely because of their adaptation to shade.

Five light-catching plants

Miscanthus sinensis
An oriental grass with feathery flowers that light up in the low autumn light.
1–1.5m x 1.2m

Chamaerops humilis
This hardy fan palm has great structural presence and will cast intriguing shadows.
1.5–2m x 1m

Lunaria annua
The translucent seed heads of this biennial look like silvery moons.
1m x 30cm

Clematis tangutica 'Bill Mackenzie'
Bears fluffy, hair-like seed heads after orange peel coloured flowers.
5m x 2m

Fatsia japonica
The large, very glossy leaves of this shade-loving plant will reflect a lot of light.
2–3m x 2–3m

TOP LEFT In this shaded spot a number of elements are working hard to maximise the available light. The vertical water feature has been made from highly reflective metal, whilst the running water and the smooth, polished paving both work to bounce back as much light as possible.

BOTTOM LEFT Here a curtain of highly reflective plastic sheets, coated with a silvery finish, acts like a wall of mirrors to improve light levels. The timber deck has been cleverly designed to match the dimensions of the plastic curtain sheets, creating the illusion that the two features are one.

ABOVE A body of water is the ultimate in light-reflective surfaces. Here a superbly executed formal pool shows not only the visual impact of water, but also – with the stepping stones that seem to float just above the surface – the striking way it can interact with its surrounding materials.

'Through its ability to enhance light and reflect the sky and its surroundings, a body of water can transform a garden space'

Shade

OPPOSITE Gardening in deep shade can seem like a daunting prospect, but there are a host of plants that will thrive in shade, many of which have beautiful architectural qualities and superb foliage texture and colour.

If there is one climatic condition guaranteed to strike fear into the heart of the gardener, it's shade. Thoughts of half-dead plants in dusty, dry soil, loitering in gloomy half light are not usually the stuff from which gardening dreams are made. But there really is no need to be scared of shade; instead, all that is required is an understanding of how to manage the conditions it brings, because there are actually thousands of plants that will thrive in it.

Shade affects the growing conditions in gardens in a number of ways. Because the soil gets less direct sunlight, it is usually slower to warm up, which affects how quickly plants start their season's growth. The lower light levels also mean that plants have to be adapted to shade in order to be able to make food by photosynthesising; plants that aren't will turn up their toes and die when thrust into the gloom and left to get on with it.

To succeed in a shady garden, use those plants that are adapted to growing in shade (there are thousands), and look at implementing strategies that may help improve light levels, such as the use of reflective materials and paint finishes. Light levels can also be boosted through the manipulation of plants – woody plants, for example, can have the bulk of their foliage thinned out to create an open branch structure that allows more light through, or hard pruned back to the ground to boost light levels at the start of the season, when many lower-growing plants need it most to start into growth.

Light-coloured or variegated foliage plants can also provide a light-boosting opportunity. A group of the silver-, white- or golden-leaved plants, such as the silvery false forget-me-not *Brunnera macrophylla* 'Jack Frost' in a dark corner can be as good as a pool of sunlight. Careful placement of variegated plants is required, however, as too many of them, especially with a mixture of golden and silver variegation, can look disastrously incoherent.

Five plants for shady gardens

Dryopteris erythrosora
This handsome border fern has bronze-pink young fronds.
60cm x 40cm

Anemone hupehensis
A lovely autumn-flowering perennial that quickly colonises in shade.
60cm x 40cm

Hakonechloa macra 'Aureola'
An attractive yet understated grass with deep green foliage.
35cm x 40cm

Galanthus nivalis
Snowdrops are one of the year's first flowers and are always a joy.
10cm x 10cm

Geranium macrorrhizum
Has fragrant foliage when crushed and attractive flowers.
50cm x 60cm

Full sun

OPPOSITE Amongst the many thousands of plants that thrive in full sun are some real specialists. *Allium* (top left) cope with drought – as do the majority of bulbous plants – by vanishing below ground before the weather gets too hot. Many of the palms, including *Chamaerops humilis* (bottom right) have a hard outer coating to their leaves, like a plastic shell, that helps them to hold on to moisture, while *Aeonium* (bottom left) have thick fleshy leaves to store water and starch.

Whilst gardens that benefit from full sun may seem easier to deal with in design terms than shaded gardens, there are actually just as many challenges to face. Materials have to be selected that aren't blindingly harsh in bright sunlight, whilst a comfortable retreat from the heat and sun for the most delicate plants has to be provided. Managing the soil can throw up challenges too, as unrelenting sunshine can cause rapid drying out, which then leads to plants wilting.

However, just as with a shady space, appropriate plant selection is key to creating a successful garden in full sun. Unsuitable plants (often those with very big, soft leaves or lots of soft, sappy growth) can wilt in minutes in a really hot garden, whilst containers will need a continuous round of watering unless they are planted with suitably drought-resistant plants, in which case they might go for weeks without a drop of water, even in really hot weather.

Strongly architectural plants such as *Yucca*, *Agave*, *Aloe* and *Chamaerops* excel as they have both the presence and the appropriate aesthetic to succeed in full sun – the glare of which brings plants and features into sharper relief and bleaches out subtle colour. These plants are at their best in the garden when used sparingly; a planting featuring a few key structural plants along with a ground storey of lower-growing plants is the best way to showcase these extreme drought specialists. It is also worth remembering that such powerful architectural plants also cast strong shadows that can be as attractive as the plants themselves when thrown against a white-painted wall or sheet of reflective water.

Five plants for full sun

Lavandula lanata
Like all lavenders, this species is a must-have for its fragrant foliage and flowers.
75cm x 90cm

Yucca gloriosa
The 'Spanish Dagger' is an imposing plant with large, sword-like leaves and huge flower spikes.
2m x 2m

Perovskia 'Blue Spire'
This upright shrub has silvery-white foliage and powder-blue flowers.
1.2m x 1m

Cistus 'Blanche'
This perrenial shrub is easy to look after, fast-growing and very colourful.
1.5m x 1.5m

Santolina chamaecyparissus
This cotton lavender makes neat, rounded bushes with finely divided foliage of silvery-white or grey-green.
2m x 2m

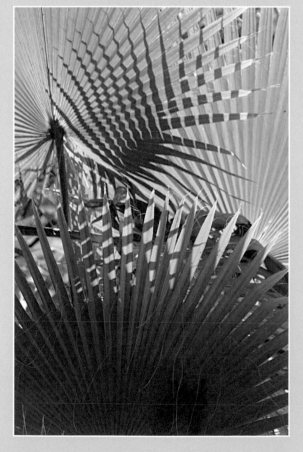

Using artificial light

BELOW Artificial lighting can be as subtle and complex as the effects created by natural light and shade. In this garden a range of lighting sources and styles have been combined to create general background light as well as targeted light to pick out specific features.

When the sun goes down, the lights need no more go out in the garden than they do indoors. Artificial lighting allows the use of the outdoor space to be maximised, extending the garden experience beyond the daylight hours, but at its best it can bring a completely new and distinct quality to the garden. Whilst natural light can be manipulated to some degree, the deployment of artificial lighting is completely in our control. At its most basic, this can be the illumination of the space to provide safe access after dark. But with considered application, artificial lighting becomes something far more significant, capable of highlighting specific features or providing a continuum from the indoor space, or creating an entirely distinct outdoor experience that emphasises the special nature of gardens after dark.

Outdoor lighting, or 'lightscaping' as it is sometimes known, can transform the experience of the garden at night. A pool of water, for example, primarily acts as a reflective body during the daytime, bouncing and amplifying light from its surface. But at night, artificial lighting placed

within the pool completely changes its nature, causing it to be a source of light, rather than a mirror to it. Artificial lighting can also be used to highlight plants or features that are largely hidden during the day – a tree, shrub or container can become the centrepiece for the entire garden with appropriate lighting. And the mode of lighting can become a feature in its own right; tea lights or candles arranged in an alcove or lined up along an outdoor dining table or floating on the surface of a pool can bring a little nocturnal magic to the garden.

ABOVE The repetition of this row of clipped evergreen shrubs becomes even more effective after dark, thanks to the addition of simple uplighters that accentuate their form and shape.

LEFT Even the most simple, low-level lighting can have an impact if it is positioned well. A double alcove with tea light holders is effective because of the uncluttered simplicity, whilst a down lighter illuminates the light-catching flowers of *Pennisetum villosum*.

Colour

Of the many reasons why humans are attracted to making and caring for gardens – the opportunity to create, the connection with the environment, healthy living and so on – a love of colour must come close to the top of the list of motivating factors. Flowers offer near-limitless colour variation, foliage less in scope but often different in tone, and the materials, paint finishes and features we use in the garden offer yet more variety. Even without flowers or other adornments, a garden will still brim with the most ubiquitous of outdoor colours – green.

A love of colour may well be one of the principal reasons for wanting to garden, but colour can also be a point on which tastes diverge wildly. Many of us will have a favourite colour, to wear or simply to admire, and a hue that we avoid at all costs. Years ago an acquaintance of mine used to restore and sell old sports cars which he would often paint in lurid shades of lime green, turquoise and vivid tangerine. His theory was simple, and often worked; whilst nine out of ten of his potential buyers would be abhorred by the garish colours, one person would fall head over heels in love and simply have to have the car.

In a garden, the use of colour is arguably even more complicated, not least because colours are rarely static or stable in this living, changing environment, affected as they are by variations in light levels and, if the colours in question are those of plants, also by their conditions. Indeed, light has the critical part to play in how we 'read'

'A love of colour may well be one of the principal reasons for wanting to garden'

ABOVE Whether complementary or contrasting, some colours seem especially well suited to one another. Here steel blue becomes even steelier when set against a foreground of rusty orange-brown.

colour, as it is wavelengths of light that we see as colour. Early and late in the day, when light is often diffused due to the relative position of the sun, many colours appear more vibrant, with blues and purples often taking on almost fluorescent qualities. It is at these times, at dusk and dawn, that garden and landscape photographers are often busiest, taking advantage of the clarity and softness of the light and the vibrancy and intensity of colour.

Hot and cold colour

OPPOSITE Blue is definitely a cold colour, as the wonderfully intense *Meconopsis grandis* (top right) demonstrates. Combined with a mixture of silvers and purples, it can form effective cool complementary plantings (bottom right). Hot colours such as vibrant red, vivid yellow and burnt orange will show well even in strong light (bottom left); whilst placing a group of hot colours together (top left) can help foreshorten vistas.

Although the colours experienced in the garden can often be complex and highly variable, for the sake of brevity and simplicity in design terms they are usually arranged under two main headings: hot or cold. Hot colours include red and its various hues, along with shades of orange and magenta. Cold colours include blue, violet, cyan and turquoise, as well as shades of green. The 'fringe' colours, yellow and purple, are variable in that they can be either hot or cold depending on the colours they are associated with. White and silver, though usually thought of as cold colours, can in fact be placed under either heading, again depending on how they are used.

Hot colours are progressive in the landscape – that is to say they usually appear closer than they actually are, thanks to the vibrancy of their hue – whilst cold colours are recessive, appearing further away. These qualities can be played with to deploy some special effects; a short garden can be made to appear longer by massing cool colours at the far boundary, whilst a long garden can be foreshortened with the use of plenty of hot colours at the end of the longest view. Various permutations of this can be applied to make wide gardens seem narrower, narrow gardens wider and so on. Whilst this technique isn't completely foolproof, by and large it works.

The way we interpret colour is influenced by light levels and background colour, which also impacts on the relative heat or coolness of colours. A mass of hot reds and purples can look dark and turgid in shaded conditions, whilst cooler colours will sing out of the gloom, providing a light contrast against their dark surroundings. For this reason, plants that rely on pollinating insects such as moths that fly at dusk and dark often have light-coloured flowers – as well as being fragrant in the evening – to act as a beacon to draw the insects in. Conversely, in really bright, sunny conditions, especially where there is a lot of reflected light, pastel shades can appear washed out and faded into blandness, whilst bold, hot colours really stand out.

'A mass of hot reds and purples can look dark and turgid in shaded conditions, whilst cooler colours will sing out of the gloom'

Complementary colour

OPPOSITE
Complementary
colour schemes have
an overwhelming
sensation of being
easy on the eye. Their
soothing, harmonious
effect is the same
whether the scheme is
hot, like this one, or
cold (below).

How we use colour in the garden will, inevitably, be heavily influenced by personal taste, but there are some opportunities and pitfalls that it helps to be aware of. Complementary colour schemes can often help to create a sense of unity and cohesion in a garden, which can be especially effective in a small space where the aim is to make the garden feel less cramped. This doesn't mean using a single colour throughout, but a range of colours that sit beside one another well; blue with purple, violet, lavender and silver, for example. The overall effect is often cool, restrained and measured, but there is no reason why a complementary colour scheme can't be hot and bold – it is entirely down to the composition and content.

A complementary colour scheme should major on subtle shifts in tone and hue rather than dramatic changes. Fortunately the flower colours of plants tend to have seemingly infinite variability; within what could be described as the colour blue, for example, are indigo, purple, lavender, sky blue, royal blue, powder blue, turquoise and so on. The same is true of pretty much every colour in the garden, even plain old green (which of course is anything but). But this variation alone is not enough to ensure that a complementary colour scheme is successful, as there needs to be some contrast otherwise the effect will be at best flat, at worst bland and forgettable

If you're a plant enthusiast and your garden is small, then the desire to have a variety of plants will often outweigh the golden rule that, by and large, less is more. If plants with similar colour qualities are grouped together, then the risk of creating a colour bombshell is avoided, with the added bonus that the space will probably seem larger, thanks to the unifying colour scheme. Repeating plants or features with the same colour can also enhance the sense of travelling on a visual journey through the garden, by drawing the eye through a composition or along a feature such as a path.

'To ensure that a complementary colour scheme is successful there needs to be some contrast or the effect will be at best flat, at worst bland and forgettable'

Contrasting colour

BELOW In this composition, from Jardin Majorelle in Marrakech, Morocco, the contrast between the deep-blue wall colour – a signature of the garden – and the eye-wateringly vibrant flowers of *Pelargonium* couldn't be more stark. But the pot colour has also been carefully selected; fresh, spearmint green being as much a contrast to the blue background as the pinkish-red flowers.

Contrasting one or a number of colours against others creates a very different feel to a complementary scheme. Done well it can bring a sense of excitement and vibrancy to proceedings, the effect of differing colours intermingling throwing up some startlingly delicious results, but when badly executed the results can end up looking like an explosion in a paint factory. To avoid this potential disaster, the most effective contrasting schemes often utilise a limited palette of different hues, with just a scattering of loud colours. But then sometimes the whole point of a contrasting scheme is to take the book of good taste and burn it in a great conflagration of clashing colours.

In some instances the plant will provide its own contrast within the confines of its flower or foliage, be it a subtle, muted combination such as the magenta petals and dark-centred flower of *Geranium psilostemon*, or more flamboyant blends like the foliage of *Actinidia kolomikta*, with its mid-green leaves splashed with white and dusky pink. But plants don't work in isolation, of course, and the integration of hard landscaping materials with the colours of flower and foliage offers plenty of opportunities to exploit. Cool, gray slate or weathered cedar, teamed with the silvery, sword-like leaves of *Astelia chathamica* can create a crisp, clean look, particularly effective in semi-shaded conditions. In brighter light the use of warmer-coloured materials will counteract the bleaching effect of the sun, a pinkish-terracotta wall can be the ideal counterpoint for blowsy, impossibly bright-coloured *Bougainvillea* flowers.

RIGHT When it comes to colour, taste can be a very subjective thing. This stained-glass window (in the cathedral of St Stephen, Budapest) is a cacophony of colour, yet somehow it still manages to be beautiful. Assembling such an array of colours together in a garden isn't always successful as so much depends on the depth of colour – the subtleties of shade and hue, the shape and size of the plants and their flowers, the light levels and so on.

ABOVE Orange and purple make for one of the best contrasting colour combinations in the garden, as the intensity of one highlights and makes more vivid the vibrancy of the other. Here the orange, papery bloom of *Papaver ruprifragum* hovers above the starry purple flowers of *Allium christophii*.

'Sometimes the whole point of a contrasting scheme is to take the book of good taste and burn it in a great conflagration of clashing colours'

Seasonal variation and intensity

OPPOSITE Autumn is the season when many plants provide a spectacular last hurrah, their leaves displaying a range of vivid colours as they undergo a process of chemical change.

Seasonal variation of colour is one of the natural highlights of both the garden, and the wider natural landscape, with certain colours and hues dominant and others recessive at various times throughout the course of the year. We're all attuned to nature's brilliance during autumn, when in a good year, and in the right place, the vibrant shades of turning foliage rivals any other natural phenomenon, but each season has its own colour 'flavour', the hues that help define it from the rest.

In the garden this seasonal variation is evident in the dominance of particular colours at different time of the year. During early spring, yellow is in the ascendance, with daffodils, pussy willow, *Mahonia* and *Forsythia* amongst the many yellow-flowered plants at their peak, before giving way to the blue of bluebells, *Salvia*, *Camassia* and alpine *Campanula*, accompanied by the almost translucent freshness of newly unfurled foliage. By summer the hotter hues take centre stage – reds, purples and violets amongst them – before autumn kicks in with golden yellow, orange and deep, burgundy red. These colours aren't dominant to the exclusion of all others, of course, but nevertheless they help give each season a distinct colour range and feeling.

'Each season has its own colour "flavour", the hues that help define it from the rest'

ABOVE Fruit trees are full of blossom in spring, creating a very distinctive seasonal display that will change as the season progresses and fruits form and begin to ripen.

For some plants the ageing process brings out a completely new dimension to the colour of the plant, or changes its colour altogether. Autumn leaf colour is a consequence of the decline of the structure of the leaf in readiness for winter, causing the green chlorophyll to dissipate and the other colours within the leaf – gold, yellow, red – to be seen. This process affects all plants, not just big forest trees, and there are plenty of grasses and perennials that are just as colourful as their bigger brethren. Autumn is also the season for colourful fruits, berries and nuts, which come into their own as leaves fall and flowers fade, many of which will persist for some months until the combination of frosts and hungry animals or foraging human hands finally sees them off. Beyond autumn and into winter the top growth of most non-woody plants dies, and so changes colour again. Ornamental grasses like *Miscanthus* and *Molinia* take on a straw-coloured hue, eventually bleaching almost to white, whilst flowering perennials turn dark brown or black, often topped with attractive seed heads that are as pretty to look at as they are important as a food source for animals.

Texture

OPPOSITE When the brightest of colours are stripped away, leaving subtler hues of green and straw-yellow, the less-celebrated qualities of texture can come into their own. Here *Allium* 'Firmament', *Stipa tenuissima* and *Geranium* 'Irish Blue' demonstrate the impact of textural contrast.

I suspect that texture is probably the last thing we think of when it comes to gardens. Colour and fragrance are probably top of the list, followed perhaps by light, and maybe space – or at least a preoccupation with the lack of it. And yet the textural qualities of plants and materials are just as important, and enjoyable, as these more obvious elements.

The term 'texture' is most often used in relation to the physical feel of an object, whether it is smooth or rough, hard or soft, sticky or dry. But texture can also refer to a compositional outcome, principally in musical terms where the effect of layers of sound or tonal variation is often described as influencing the 'texture' of a piece. The term, with this meaning, is equally applicable in the garden, where the interaction between the various components that make up the whole (say the combination of soft, silky oriental grasses with the coarse surfaces of igneous basalt rock) can have a sense of cohesion that is the visual equivalent of an orchestral symphony.

'The various components that make up the whole can have a sense of cohesion that is the visual equivalent of an orchestral symphony'

Plants offer plenty of textural interaction in their foliage, flowers and stems, with every experience on offer from rabbit soft to razor sharp, rough as sandwood to slippery as patent leather. Hard landscaping materials have just as much to offer texturally. A smooth, diamond-cut slab of sandstone or a piece of dressed slate will be just as irresistible to touch as a soft, velvety leaf. And the texture of hard materials can also change according to the weather conditions; little pools of water will collect in roughly dressed stone, but roll off smoother finishes, for example.

To me the tactile qualities of objects and plants are just as pleasurable as the visual and olfactory, but it isn't just how things feel texturally that matters in a garden; it's how texture changes the look of things too, and in turn how this influences the scale of a space. The influence of textural changes in a space, though often subtle, can be highly effective. A few years ago a study was made into the effect of paving surfaces on burglary rates in residential estates. It found that replacing tarmac with coloured block paving discouraged people from going beyond a certain point. The coloured paving created an effective visual, though not physical, barrier. In a garden, similar textural tricks can be played out too: changing the scale of paving materials from large, smoothly finished paving stones to smaller, more detailed paving such as a stable yard paver (about the size of a brick but divided further into six raised squares) can encourage a slowing down, or dictate a change of direction in a path.

Texture in plants

Some plants just cry out to be touched. The flowers of the grass *Pennisetum villosum* are as soft as cotton wool, the leaves of lamb's ear (*Stachys byzantina*) are like crushed velvet, whilst another grass, *Stipa tenuissima*, is quite rightly known as the hair grass, as its leaves are as fine and pliable as a fulsome head of hair.

These tactile qualities are not the result of the plant's desire to be fondled of course, rather a consequence of the need to adapt to particular climatic or regional conditions. The nap of thick hairs on the leaves of lamb's ear form a protective barrier that traps moisture from the air and reduces water loss, whilst the needle-thin leaves of hair grass are as narrow as they are to prevent excess water loss. Extreme drought specialists need to carry as much moisture as possible in their leaves, stems or roots, which often become swollen with sap and starch as a result. *Aloe vera* and *Agave americana*, for example, have thick, fleshy leaves that feel more like polished wood, plastic, or old, burnished leather to the touch than living plant material. Other plants have adopted the trick of keeping their leaves and even their flowers covered with a thin layer of wax, sticky enough to feel noticeably tacky to the touch, in order to prevent water loss from wind.

Some plants have developed textural qualities further – into defensive armour, forming spines, barbs and thorns. The formidable *Colletia paradoxa*

'*Aloe vera* and *Agave americana* have thick, fleshy leaves that feel more like polished wood, plastic, or old, burnished leather to the touch than living plant material'

has entirely disposed of conventional foliage and instead has flattened stems equipped with fearsome spines, whilst a huge array of cacti have tooled up with monstrous barbs and thorns designed to challenge all but the most tenacious of herbivores. While these plants may not be top of the touchy-feely list, there is no doubting they bring a strikingly different textural dimension to the garden.

Flowers are as texturally variable as foliage; however, their tactile qualities are often overlooked, perhaps as a result of their striking visual qualities. Rose petals have the most exquisitely silky feel, whilst the central boss of *Echinacea* has a stiff, bristly quality. The bottlebrush plant *Callistemon rigidus* has soft, brush-like blooms that are soft to the touch and are wonderfully exotic to look at, whilst other flowers, such as *Bracteantha bracteata* (known as the golden everlasting daisy) have a papery texture that feels more like parchment than plant.

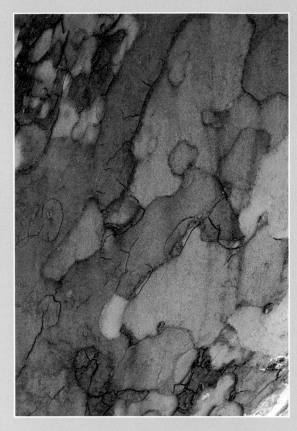

LEFT Some *Allium* flower heads are very large, about the size of a grapefruit, but each is comprised of masses of smaller individual flowers that are loved by bees and that give the plant its distinctive textural quality.

LEFT *Echinops* flowers have a wonderfully tactile quality. Dry and rather stiff to the touch, the individual petals spring back into place when rubbed with a finger.

ABOVE The most obviously visible part of the *Bougainvillea* flower is in fact a bract, which has a very distinctive papery texture that contributes to its long-lasting colour in the garden – in effect it is a living dried flower.

RIGHT *Nigella damascena* has a papery quality to its flowers, but also incredibly fine, filigree foliage that gives the whole plant a floating, gossamer-like texture that contributes to its aesthetic suitability for cottage garden plantings.

LEFT The flowers of the aptly named bottlebrush plant *Callistemon rigidus*, an Australian native, are perfectly described by the common name, both in shape but also in texture, which is like a soft brush.

LEFT The flowers of *Astrantia major* are comprised of white- or pink-tinged bracts that have a stiff, papery texture and surround the flower. These bracts are designed to make the plant more attractive to pollinating insects by making the flower seem bigger and therefore more worth a visit – it's the plant world's equivalent of an advertising hoarding.

Texture and materials

If you've ever been on a country walk and have crossed an old-fashioned timber stile, your hand will probably have rested on a wooden upright so well worn by thousands of preceding hands that it was as polished and smooth as a chestnut. A few inches further along the stile, the near virgin wood, untroubled by all that handling, will likely be almost as rough to the touch as it was when it left the mill. It's just one small example of how the texture of materials can change; in this case through repeated handling, but also from weathering and from different treatments during manufacture that lead to a variety of textural finishes.

RIGHT Using hard landscaping materials with different textural qualities and sizes is an effective way of altering scale in the garden. Here a smooth-finished paving stone gives way to a much rougher-hewn granite sett, in a variety of sizes, which in turn yields to a timber deck.

LEFT Using the same material in different forms can help to unify the garden by providing continuity of materials whilst also giving different textural qualities. Here slate is used in two forms: smooth finished paving stones for walking on, and small crushed shards as a mulch for plants.

125

Vision

BELOW The contrast between the solidity of the timber comprising this raised bed, and the soft, billowing grass overhanging it, makes for a very effective composition. The rusted iron capping is a nice design touch that adds another textural dimension.

Stone is an extremely versatile hard material which can be worked in a number of ways to create a variety of textural effects – a good understanding of which opens up the possibilities for their repeated use as part of the composition of the design throughout the garden. The finish of different types of stone also affects its light-reflecting qualities and the rate at which it sheds or holds water, which in turn changes its appearance and colour – wet slate, for example, has a glossy, almost oily appearance that changes significantly when it is dry and takes on a slightly chalky hue.

The texture of timber is similarly affected by the manner in which it is finished. A milled, planed oak post has a smooth, precise quality suitable for an application where clean lines are important, whereas the same piece of timber, split and roughly finished, will have a far more rustic feel, ideal for a country garden or the boundary between a cultivated space and the wild ground beyond. Similarly, timber also changes its textural quality through weathering, with raw softwood losing some of its roughness thanks to the gradual softening by wind, sun and rain; whilst perhaps one of the most dramatic examples of the manner in which materials can change is the way that green oak (oak timber that is sawn and dressed whilst still 'wet' with sap) develops 'shakes', cracks and fissures that appear along and across the grain of the wood over time.

Combining textures

BELOW Combining the relative textural qualities of plants and hard landscaping materials opens up all sorts of design possibilities to exploit. Deeply cut fern fronds can complement the small-scale complexity of a pebble mosaic path (left), whilst large slate paving stones can provide an effective contrast with interlacing panels of tiny-leaved creeping plants such as *Soleirolia soleirolii* (right).

The textural interaction between different hard landscaping materials, their various finishes and the plants around them is also significant. Smooth, highly finished stone, laid in geometrically precise lines, takes on a strong, contemporary air when paired with strongly architectural plants like grasses, exotic palms, glossy-leaved evergreen shrubs or succulents. Conversely, a meandering gravel path with uneven width along its length will, when combined with the softer, smaller or deeply-cut foliage of cottage garden plants such as *Nigella damascena*, *Delphinium* and *Lupinus* result in a far more informal, relaxed look.

Mixing different textures can also create an interesting aesthetic tension, or help to soften or sharpen a feature. A large 'statement' rock, placed in the bend of a path or at the end of a vista, will have a distinctive character if left uncluttered as a monolith to be enjoyed in its own right, but when planted with an airy, soft-textured grass such as *Nassella trichotoma*, *Hordeum jubatum* or *Eragrostis airoides*, it takes on the role of a dynamic textural counterpoint.

Crevice planting offers an opportunity to closely combine the different qualities of stone and plants, using small-leaved succulent plants such as *Sempervirens*, planted in between the crevices formed by standing slate or sandstone on edge, which are then packed out with growing media. The succulents quickly colonise around the crevice stone so that the two appear to be a single entity. Likewise, containers can be selected for their ability to contrast or complement the texture of the plants within them; a copper pan, smooth-textured but with the textural and colour patina of verdigris, can be combined with the bronze-leaved, low-growing *Sedum*, which complements the patina of the pot whilst providing a counterpoint to it, thanks to the size and glossy finish of the foliage.

The passage of time, and the effect of foot traffic, handling and weathering all alter the textures of stone and timber too, softening out hard edges and encouraging the colonisation of the ultimate textural softener – and indeed the most natural and effortless combination of plants and materials – mosses, algae and lichen.

LEFT In Tom Hoblyn's Chelsea Flower Show garden, timber wave forms contrast strongly with large 'pebbles' (in fact cushions designed to look like stone). The garden was later rebuilt as part of Clive and Debbie's Suffolk garden.

BELOW The coarse vertical foliage of *Equisetum hyemale* creates a textural curtain behind this beautifully executed rill, and contrasts with the hard materials of cut stone and crushed slate that comprise it, as well as the smooth pebble stepping stones beyond.

Shape and form

OPPOSITE
Sometimes the simplest features make the boldest statements in the garden. Here the combination of strongly contrasting colour and bold shape and form are all that is needed to make an arresting composition.

A shape is an enclosed area, distinct and distinguished from its surroundings and usually considered to be two-dimensional; it has height and width. Form, by contrast, is the organisation of visual elements into three dimensions; in addition to height and width, form has depth – or at least the illusion of depth. A knowledge of the many different shapes and forms that can be found within the garden is as crucial to the success of your design as an understanding of colour or texture, and will help to bring a sense of dynamism and life into a space.

Amongst the many factors that affect our perception of shape and form is the viewpoint or position from where we see an object, which can highlight certain features and obscure others. This can change as we move around an object, getting closer to it or further away, or viewing it obliquely or head on. It is also the visual phenomenon that, in part, is exploited by *trompe l'oeil* (trick of the eye), where a flat surface, often a wall, is painted to appear as a three-dimensional object, often as an outdoor view to create the illusion that a space is much larger than it actually is.

The character and content of the space around an object can also affect how we perceive shape and form. A solitary oak tree, standing tall in an open landscape, has far more visual impact than an oak tree in a wood, where it becomes absorbed as part of the fabric of the whole. Likewise, a garden seat, as part of a group, is understood to be merely one item in a set of furniture, whereas separated out and positioned at the end of a vista it instead becomes a focal point, or 'eye-catcher'.

Light too has a crucial role to play in how we perceive shape and form. If an object has a smooth side and a rough side and is lit head on, both textural qualities will be apparent. But if lit from the smooth side, the rough side will be in deep shadow and to all intents invisible. Light can also change the character of an object by making it appear more or less worn and aged, with softer, head-on lighting far more flattering than hard, shadow-casting side lighting.

Core plant shapes

ABOVE The daisy flowers of plants from the Asteraceae family, such as *Echinacea* are amongst the most recognisable of all flower shapes.

There are a number of core shapes that are recognised in plants, and a good understanding of these will enable you to combine them in ways that will lend maximum visual impact to your garden.

Fastigiated, columnar or pencil-shaped plants, such as *Taxus baccata* 'Fastigiata', with their upright, relatively tight forms, create strong dominant outlines within the garden. These are the shapes that make a statement and can be used to create 'punctuation' (marking the beginning or end of a path or a gateway) to frame a vista, or to create a sense of rhythm in a space through their repetition. At the opposite end of the shape scale are the creeping, horizontal plants that grow outward along the ground rather than upright. These plants have many useful practical applications; they are good for covering ground and suppressing weeds and also help form the important lower level for the overall composition of a planting scheme. In between these two groups are a variety of spreading, arching and cascading shapes, which can be useful for everything from filling space (forming natural alternatives to topiary) to making a graceful focal 'pinch point' or turn in a planting that encourages you to look around the corner.

At a much more detailed level are the shapes and forms that comprise a plant's individual flowers and foliage. From the classic daisy to the complex, bilateral symmetry of orchid blooms, flowers have distinct, often beautiful shapes. Mixing these differing shapes can be an effective way of adding life and interest into your garden, with clever combinations such as the marrying of *Echinacea*'s fat, daisy flowers with the slender flower spikes of the powder-blue *Perovskia* 'Blue Spire', or the mixing of cascading blooms of *Laburnum* with plump, round *Allium* flower heads providing the little touch that can lift your garden from the mundane to the sublime.

5 plants with distinct shapes

Malus sargentii
A lovely, slow-growing, small-spreading tree with white blossom and red fruit.
4m x 5m

Armeria maritima
Forms a tight bun of foliage with pretty pink flowers.
20cm x 30cm

Cotoneaster horizontalis
This low-growing shrub spreads outward parallel to the ground.
1m x 1.5m

Calamagrostis emodensis
A beautiful grass with pretty, arching flowers.
60cm x 60cm

Cupressus sempervirens
Pencil-thin and tall, this is the quintessential tree of the Tuscan countryside.
15–20m x 1–6m

LEFT The vertical flower spikes of plants like the foxtail lily, *Eremurus*, can be used to create the vertical element in a planting, or celebrated for their shape, form and presence by allowing them the space to stand out alone.

'Mixing differing flower shapes can be an effective way of adding life and interest into your garden'

Manipulating plant shapes

OPPOSITE Fruit trees are pruned and trained for aesthetic, practical and cultural reasons; elaborate pruning styles such as this freestanding pyramid restrict the overall size of the plant, improve fruiting by encouraging lots of lateral flowering wood, and also make a very effective feature plant.

RIGHT Some plants have the capacity to take pruning and training to such an extent that they can become quite unlike the plant in its native state, as these pad-pruned hornbeam *Carpinus betulus* demonstrate.

Along with the exploitation of naturally occurring plant shapes, the manipulation of plants by pruning and training offers another level of opportunity for creativity in the garden. Perhaps the most common form of garden plant manipulation is the planting and shaping of hedgerows. Whilst these are regularly pruned into roughly 'A'-sectioned shapes and used as boundary-marking rectilinear forms, by planting and cutting them to create interlocking shapes of varying heights they can instead be made to frame a particular vista or object, or sculpted into visually intriguing, undulating shapes or serpentine forms.

Individual plants can also come under the influence of the clippers to

interesting effect. Topiary has something of a mixed reputation – historically evocative and impressive in execution when seen in an appropriately grand location, it can seem out of place and twee in suburbia unless executed with absolute conviction and skill. But the less extreme version of topiary, where plants are clipped into strongly architectural shapes as opposed to stylised objects, can be highly effective at creating the same kind of effects of punctuation, framing and repetitive rhythm that can be found when using plants which naturally possess distinctively strong form.

There are almost no limits to the ways in which plants can be manipulated into seemingly impossible shapes. Street trees are often dramatically pruned not just to restrict their growth but also to provide a suitable amount of shade. Climbing plants such as roses, vines and climbing hydrangea are usually trained against wires on a timber or steel framework in order to enhance their flowering, fruiting or simply to support their growth; whilst fruit trees are commonly trained so that they can be accommodated into smaller spaces – often (particularly with the more elaborate forms of espalier training) with the most strikingly effective aesthetic results.

'There are almost no limits to the ways in which plants can be trained and manipulated into seemingly impossible shapes'

ABOVE The garden at East Ruston Old Vicarage in Norfolk makes great use of formal topiary shapes contrasted with loose, billowing grasses. Here, clipped box pyramids and box balls frame a central topiary holly, all softened by ornamental grasses and bold orange *Dahlia*.

RIGHT Two huge blocks of yew (*Taxus baccata*) stand like sentinels either side of the top of this flight of steps, the ascent of which is echoed in the clipped box to either side that steps up in concert with the risers of the stone steps. The combined effect magnifies the impact of what would otherwise be a fairly modest feature, turning it into something with significant presence.

LEFT Repeated clipped box balls, so closely planted as to appear connected to one another, create an undulating sea of topiary that is further amplified by dappled sunlight.

Fragrance and sound

Whilst the most obvious pleasures of a garden – colour, form and texture – may well be the easiest to express visually and are therefore the ones we often consider first and foremost, fragrance and sound are just as vital in contributing to our overall sensual enjoyment of the garden. Whether experienced up close with a nose pressed against the flower of a pungent beauty, or as a scent caught on the air, the source an unseen mystery that invites greater exploration, fragrant plants are one of the garden's true joys. And though we seek refuge in their supposed 'quiet', gardens are far from silent. Instead they are alive with the sounds of buzzing insects, birdsong, the trickle of a water feature or the rustle of the wind blowing through the foliage of an ornamental grass or the leaves of a tree.

The enhancement of these two sensual pleasures within your outdoor space can often be the result of other changes you will have instigated, for a variety of reasons, in the process of making your garden. Encouraging wildlife into the garden by planting pollen- and nectar-rich plants in the garden will attract more bees, butterflies and moths to arrive; whilst putting out bird seed, erecting nest boxes and resisting the urge to use chemicals to control pests will see more birds descending upon the garden in pursuit of prey, seed or habitat, as well as ensuring that there is a greater chance of them hanging around. Including more fragrant plants in the garden makes perfect sense, not least because in many cases the most fragrant plants are often also those that are rich in pollen and nectar, covering two desirable outcomes at once: a beautifully fragrant garden and a host of handsome insects that will visit and enjoy them. And creating features that are designed to make a noise, either to help block out a louder, unwanted sound or simply to be enjoyed as a pleasure in their own right, should always be a consideration when designing a garden.

Fragrance

OPPOSITE When placing fragrant plants in the garden, try to keep the nose-to-bloom distance at a minimum by choosing a location – a house wall near the kitchen door, by a seating area or, as here, on an arch – where you will enjoy them most.

Smell is the human sense most associated with memory, so it is unsurprising that we value fragrance in plants highly and often seek out fragrant plants in favour of those without scent, even if they may be slightly poorer in terms of flower colour or size. Plants produce scent as a means of attracting the insects that many of them rely on to unknowingly pollinate their blooms. Consequently there are some plants that have developed especially powerful fragrance at particular times of the day, or specific times of year, to ensure that the right type of pollinator is wooed. Night-scented stocks (*Matthiola bicornis*) and evening primrose (*Oenothera* species) both belt out their fragrance as night falls to attract the last of the day-flying insects to stop for one last sup before they head home, and also to ensure the first moths on the wing are given a good reason to visit them first. Winter-flowering plants, like winter sweet (*Chimonanthus praecox*) and *Viburnum farreri* have to cast their scent over a long distance to ensure that, on the odd dry, sunny winter day whatever pollinators emerge – principally bumblebees and species of moth – are made aware that a feast is available.

Although insects are the intended beneficiaries of flower fragrance, we too can profit from their generosity. The key to placing fragrant plants in the garden is to put them where they are most likely to be enjoyed. A sunny seating area is the perfect location for surrounding with swathes of lavender, for example, as both the flower and foliage can be enjoyed, with a leisurely pass of the hand. Old-fashioned climbing roses, like *Rosa* 'Paul's Himalayan Musk' may only have a brief flowering period, but it's a pungent one, and this rose is perfect for training over an archway or beneath the first-floor windows of a house. As lovely as scent is in the garden, it's even better wafting into the house, so clustering fragrant plants near the house doors will ensure at least some of their smell permeates the home. This is particularly important with winter- and spring-flowering subjects that, during prolonged periods of poor weather, might be completely overlooked unless they are close enough to be enjoyed through an open window or door.

'The key to placing fragrant plants in the garden is to put them where they are most likely to be enjoyed'

Sound

OPPOSITE
Ornamental grasses are amongst the finest garden plants for bringing sound to the garden, either when in active green growth or during autumn and winter when they begin to dry and become more straw-like.

ABOVE Sound in the garden can come from a variety of sources, some of which, like water features, are controllable, whilst others like wind chimes or the chatter of birdsong are less easy to manage, but equally valued.

Though few of us ever get the opportunity to appreciate the luxury that is a complete absence of sound, we all strive to escape from the hubbub of modern living from time to time. Whilst indoors we can shield ourselves from unwanted noise with double glazing, thick curtains, insulated walls and snug-fitting doors, in our gardens there is no such barrage of barriers to block out the aural intrusion.

Planting rows of trees and hedges in attempt to screen out excessive noise is, thanks to the way that sound waves travel, of limited or no effect. Though the sound might be slightly muted or disrupted, screening out loud noise adequately would require very deep planting indeed. Instead, often the best way to block out unpleasant background noise is to create an alternative, diversionary sound – a 'foreground' noise that you actively want to listen to. Within the garden the principal means for doing this are with water and plants.

Running-water features need great care to get the sound levels right. Too much water flow and the volume can be too loud, leading to the sound becoming overwhelming. Too little flow and not only will the purpose be lost, the noise can become another source of irritation. A well set-up waterfall or fountain will ideally create an even sound that is loud enough to be enjoyed but not so loud as to be intrusive. There are other ways to create diversionary sounds with water too, an exotic example being the Japanese *shishi odoshi* – traditional bamboo rod bird scarers that seesaw with water, tipping into a stone bowl with their distinctive 'tuk' sound.

Plants can create sound in the garden too, but only in concert with the wind. Ornamental grasses and bamboos are well regarded for their aural qualities, creating a noise not unlike the rushing of water as the wind passes through their foliage. The wind can also be harnessed to create sound with

calming wind chimes and Aeolian harps, though these need very careful handling if you want to avoid creating a continuous cacophony of noise, or something overly kitsch.

However, perhaps the most interesting sounds in the garden are those that aren't intentionally noisy, as such, but help form a part of the overall composition. The crunch of gravel under foot, the explosive pop of the drying seed pod of a Californian poppy, or the languid buzzing of a fat bumblebee – these sounds alone give reason for making a garden.

REALISATION

3

'*One who plants a garden, plants happiness*'
Anon, Chinese proverb.

The physical making of a garden can be a lifetime process, the gradual accretion of knowledge invested back into the garden in the form of a series of improvements and developments that can be never-ending. Essentially this continuity is what, by nature, gives the garden its beauty, pleasure and spirit. The novelist and gardener H.E. Bates wrote that '*the garden that is finished is dead*' and he was absolutely right. A garden can never be finished; all the time there are plants growing and dying, seasons changing, natural weathering taking place, personal taste and circumstances developing and changing, not to mention all the many changes that are occurring to the external environment, whether as a result of property development within the area, or as a result of inevitable climate change.

Having read the 'Thought Process' section of this book you will already be aware of all the practical requirements you have for your garden, and will have also formed a good idea of which desirable elements you would like to include. The realisation process brings together these considerations, informed by an understanding of the components that comprise the garden experience described in the 'Vision' section, to make a whole. Though this might sound relatively easy and straightforward, in practice it is a venture full of potential pitfalls and tricky questions, because making a garden is, for most of us, as out of our day-to-day experience as rewiring a house or plumbing in a new bathroom. However, so long as you are armed with a simple understanding of how to go about turning your dreams into reality, there's no doubting that it can not only be great fun, but also hugely rewarding.

The key to minimising potential problems and maximising the enjoyment of the process is in preparation and planning, whether you undertake all or part of the work on your own, or with the support and expertise of a professional designer. Putting the practical and desirable elements of the garden into some kind of deliverable order to ensure that making one part of the plan happen doesn't have a negative impact on, or even preclude, another part of the plan taking shape is vital. Without a plan it is all too easy to make mistakes, as some of the garden owners in *Landscape Man* found out. Even with a plan, and the support of a designer and the range of professionals that are employed in making a garden, things can, and often do, go wrong. Sometimes this can be the result of a simple mistake – Clive and Debbie's hornbeam avenue being incorrectly plotted out led to the whole tree avenue needing to be dug up and moved – other times, as in Anne and Geoff's case, a change of plan was necessitated as a result of the local planning authority refusing permission for certain proposed design elements. Whatever the reason for change, however, by having a plan in the first place you will able to clearly see the impact that one event has upon another, giving you the best opportunity to take the appropriate steps to put things right.

With a deliverable plan to work to, as well as a clear idea of what it is you want from your garden (and what you don't) there is every chance that you will be embarking on the beginning of what could be a long and extremely rewarding journey. And as your garden develops and grows, and elements wither and die as must always be with a garden, you will be given endless opportunities to redress those elements that don't work, to enhance those that do, and to accommodate changing needs. It's rare for mistakes to be made in a garden that cannot be resolved, and on occasion it is these mistakes which make the garden more interesting and are what help us to learn – although I always immodestly claim that such happy accidents are by design! This is what makes gardens, and gardening, such a rewarding exercise, providing you with as many challenges and opportunities as you want to take on and allowing as much rein to your imagination as you are willing to give.

Going it alone or engaging a designer?

Throughout the history of gardening there has been a generous smattering of knowledgeable and enthusiastic amateurs who, by establishing an overarching philosophy for their gardens and driving their development intelligently, have created great gardens on their own. Indeed, if you have the confidence and knowledge to design and realise your own garden plans then this can be an incredibly rewarding experience.

But what exactly do you need to know in order to be able to make your own garden a success? To an extent, the level of knowledge required to develop and execute your own plans depends on the type of garden you desire. A garden dominated by hard landscaping with minimalist planting, for example, will need a thorough understanding of the qualities of the materials you intend to use and the ways they can be composed on the ground to best complement each other, as well as an ability to demonstrate restraint in execution. Conversely, if you want a plant-filled garden, then you'll need an understanding of what will and won't grow where, what to do to provide optimum growing conditions, as well as having the confidence to compose with them to make the best use of colour, texture, form and shape.

The accrual of the knowledge required to plan a garden of any type can take time, whilst the ability to visualise it and then make it happen can be something that comes naturally to some people and not to others. But for every great garden made solely by its owner is a garden made by a designer working under the benefaction of an enlightened patron. Of the six gardens featured in *Landscape Man*, Keith and Ros were the only owners not to actively seek the help of a designer, and even though Keith is a professional gardener with more than 30 years' experience, he still sought assistance and employed craftsmen for those elements of the garden development that he felt were outside his skills. Clive and Debbie, Anne and Geoff and Sarah and Trevor all sought help from professional garden designers to create plans for their gardens and help project-manage the realisation stage, whilst Jason and Demetra and Vanessa and Ed had design advice from me, as well as additional assistance from a number of specialists and craftsmen.

So what are the pros and cons of going it alone versus employing a designer? A designer will of course cost money, their fees usually based on a percentage of the total contract value, this after having developed draft plans, often just sketches, which are usually done 'at risk' — i.e. the designer takes a punt that you will like what they are proposing and decide to engage them to take the work forward. Some gardeners do not charge for an initial consultation, some do. Personally, I would think twice about parting with any money 'up front' before you see what the designer is proposing.

In return for the designer's fees, you will gain a huge amount of expertise and support through the design and realisation process, which can be worth several times more than the fees charged in peace of mind and ease of process, and might actually end up as a quantifiable cash saving too, as a designer should be able to foresee many of the potential pitfalls and risks that can come with any project. A designer will also be able to take whatever ideas you have gathered, be they a simple list of likes and dislikes or more developed thoughts, and interpret and embellish them in their brief.

Working with a designer will also bring with it the wealth of contacts, craftsmen and contractors that he or she has assembled over the course of their career, taking away another time-consuming aspect of garden realisation, the trawl in search of reliable contractors that can often feel like a lottery. A really good designer will be able to hold your hand throughout the process of making your garden from brief to completion, and as such I would always recommend seeking out their help even if for only part of the process.

Budgeting

Through a lack of understanding of the total price of the elements that go into making a garden, many projects go way over budget or fall short of expectations. Usually this is due to unrealistic costing of the various components that combine to make the whole, rather than one specific area. Breaking your budget down into the following sub-sections (where relevant) should ensure that you should have every angle covered:

The site survey
Consultation, design, specification and possible project management/overseeing
Structural engineer for any complex or major construction work
Site clearance including debris removal (skip hire etc.)
Site infrastructure works (drainage, services etc.)
Hard landscaping (materials and labour)
Soft landscaping (including turf, plants and labour)
Soil preparation
Accessories such as lighting, irrigation, sheds, furniture, water features etc.

Putting it all together

If you decide not to use the services of a designer, or have a design drawn up and then choose to progress the realisation of the design yourself, the time will come when you will need to take the ideas, needs and desires for your garden from whatever paper form they take and make them happen on the ground. Ideally you'll have two paper documents from which your garden will spring — a drawing, and an action plan. The drawing can be as simple or as complex as you want it to be, from a 'back of a fag packet' sketch to a fully detailed, modelled, AutoCad (a computer-aided design) drawing that can be manipulated on-screen and stripped back or built up in layers to reveal different elements of the plan.

In some cases an AutoCad plan can be complete overkill, where all that is required is a simple planting plan, or a sketch that shows the relative positions of features that are 'self-designing', such as an off-the-shelf patio paving kit or a garden shed. But in other cases a plan of great detail can be essential, especially if dealing with complex level changes and where they relate to things like the damp-proof course of a house or existing drainage systems. If your garden requires the sort of detailing required by an AutoCad plan, then it makes complete sense to call in a professional designer, who will organise a survey of the garden before developing a plan drawing.

Creating a sketch plan

If all you need is a simple sketch plan, then it's possible to do it yourself, and if so then you'll need to start by making a basic survey of the site. To carry out a basic survey, you need a sheet of graph paper, two long tape measures, two wooden marker pegs and a hank of ranging line (which you can buy from a builders merchant). Find the longest distance between two points in your garden that can be measured in a straight line — often the boundary of the garden formed by a fence, wall or hedge — measure it and draw it on the graph paper, and ideally mark it on the ground too, with the two marker pegs and ranging line. This is what is known as the A–B line, and from it you can measure off, with a reasonable degree of accuracy, all the main fixed objects in the garden — existing paths, plants, walls, sheds and so on. This basic survey will give you such information as the overall size of your garden in square metres and the relative positions of major features, onto which you can draw whatever new features you have decided on — a new seating area, plantings, and so on. Over the next few pages you'll find examples of sketches that I have made for various gardens, some of which have then needed further, more detailed plans; others have been realised just with a pencil sketch. Take time with the drawing stage, experimenting

Measuring/Surveying

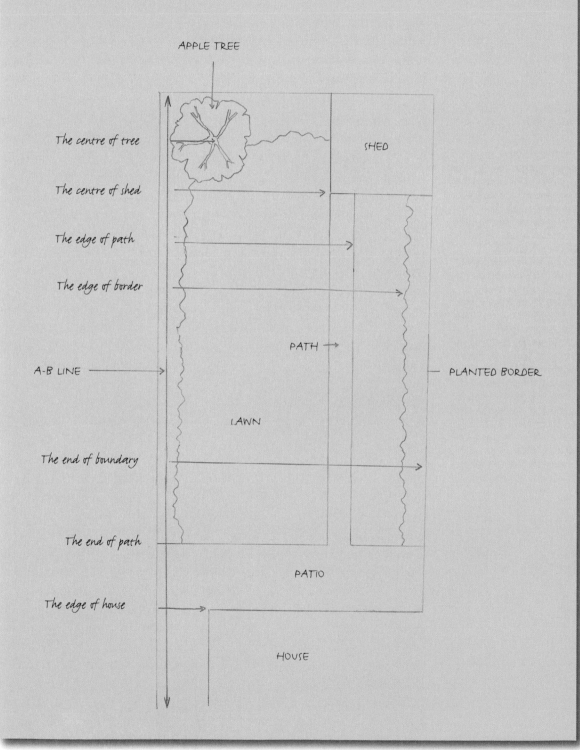

APPLE TREE

The centre of tree

The centre of shed

SHED

The edge of path

The edge of border

PATH

A-B LINE

PLANTED BORDER

LAWN

The end of boundary

The end of path

PATIO

The edge of house

HOUSE

with different approaches to each feature that you want to include, before settling on a final version. Most professional designers will spend a great deal of time working up ideas in pencil and ink before taking them further to a drawing board or AutoCad.

When you come to plotting out where the new features will go on the ground, you can use the A–B line to accurately position them by measuring

RIGHT This sample action plan for laying a patio covers all the necessary steps from researching the designs to laying the surface itself. When laying a patio surface, remember that if the maximum depth of excavation is more than 80cm you will need to check for underground services by getting a copy of the building services plan for your house from one of the utilities providers, or hiring a portable CAT scan device. If you are in any doubt at all about what lies beneath the surface, then don't dig!

Sample Action Plan – Laying a Patio

1. Research patio designs/materials online and through suppliers' catalogues.

2. Finalise design and sketch onto plan.

3. Measure out your new patio on the ground from sketch plan.

4. Visually check for any underground services (e.g. manhole covers!).

5. Estimate sub-base materials by multiplying overall size of patio (e.g. 20 sq m) with depth of sub-base (e.g. 30cm). Allow for an extra 5%.

6. Estimate finished surface materials.

7. Place orders for both sub-base and final surface, geotextile underlay, and for sand and cement or environmentally sustainable alternative (e.g. ScotAsh).

8. Book hire of cement mixer and wacker plate compactor.

9. Work out whether you will be using excavated spoil. If not cost in disposal.

10. Mark out patio, double-check and then excavate.

11. Install plastic duct pipes (x 2) under the patio for any future cabling.

12. Install geotextile fabric underlay to stop water/spoil transfer from sub base to soil.

13. Lay sub-base, consolidating in layers with wacker plate compactor.

14. Lay the final patio surface.

LEFT This computer generated sketch plan for Thomas Hoblyn's Chelsea garden demonstrates the benefits of 3D programmes in creating a detailed representation of a finished garden.

off from it, and then using something like a line marker paint (from a builders merchant) or dry sand to plot how each feature looks. Don't be afraid to make adjustments to the plan at the marking-out stage, as the visual impact of a feature can only ever be fully assessed on the ground, not on a paper plan.

Drawing up an action plan

An action plan is in essence a check list of what needs doing, and when. This might sound blindingly obvious but unless you have really thought through how to do things, and in what order, all sorts of nasty errors can crop up. A typical mistake, and one that I have made myself more than once, is to lay the base – or worse still the finished surface – of a patio only to realise that you should have put in a water pipe or electricity cable, to run a water feature or lighting. The resulting digging up of a section of perfectly laid patio, which almost never seems to go back down again properly, will remind you forever more of the need for an action plan. Likewise an action plan will prevent you from unnecessarily redoing work over and again. There's not much point in spending hours digging over borders if you then need to walk all over them to install the timbers for a pergola or put up a shed.

An action plan doesn't need to be a great big, in-depth document – it can be like a shopping list, or perhaps more accurately a holiday luggage list – just a simple A to B plan that helps to ensure that you get to where you want to go with your plans with the minimum of fuss and costly mistakes.

Realised gardens

Case Study Suffolk

**OPPOSITE Chelsea
Flower Show
gardens such as
Thomas Hoblyn's
2009 garden are
designed to delight
and inspire for a very
brief period of time –
the week long
duration of the show.
But although
ephemeral, the
realisation of such
gardens is the result
of meticulous
planning and
painstakingly
detailed construction
and planting.**

The following 32 pages illustrate a number of different 'realised' gardens in both sketch and completed, photographed form. The sketches have all been made as part of the design process, as a simple means of expressing the design concepts that were then considered for the finished garden. In some cases the sketches were worked up further and replaced by more detailed, modelled plans; in others, the ideas were taken and mapped out on the ground without additional development.

Regardless of how good an artist you may or may not be, sketching out your ideas over the graph paper survey you have made of your garden (*see Creating a sketch plan, page* 148) really is the best way to help you to focus your thoughts and consider what works and what doesn't, as well as allowing you to address such issues as scale, proportion and balance between various components. This is much easier to do than marking your plans out straight into the garden would be, and alterations are certainly much simpler to make with a pencil eraser than when something has already been built on the ground!

Each of the garden sketches is also accompanied by an additional drawing that picks out a particular planting scheme within that garden. The suggested plant combinations here have been chosen both to look good together and to fulfil a specific aesthetic quality in keeping with the design of the overall garden space, as well as being suitable for each garden's particular growing conditions.

Urban modern The design for this small city garden needed to work hard and be well organised in order to deliver the desired effect of a stylish contemporary space that can accommodate outdoor dining, structural planting, a number of different seating opportunities and a degree of privacy from the surrounding properties. The result is understated but effective, and a space that should be easy to live with for years to come whilst not so minimalist as to be unchanging or lacking energy.

2. SCREENING
A row of three olive trees, *Olea europaea*, create a strong structural presence along one boundary of the garden. The repetition helps to create a sense of harmonious unity, whilst the verticality of the trees helps to screen out the adjoining garden.

1. SEATING This bespoke table and benches comprise the most significant feature in the garden, as is often the case in smaller spaces. Consequently it is far more than just a place to sit, as it is also a focal point and structural device – so the need for it to be as attractive as possible is obvious. Here the elliptical table and benches nestle together in a cohesive, and visually neat way.

4. GRAVEL
The central area of the garden, where traditionally a lawn would be, is occupied by a low-maintenance granite-chip gravel surface which can be used as an additional seating/dining area. By retaining the shape and size of where a lawn would once have been, the balance of the garden is maintained.

5. PAVING The variety of paving surfaces in this garden helps to give textural interest, changes in scale and also avoids the sensation of a 'concrete garden', which can be an unfortunate side effect of making a hard landscaping, heavy, low-maintenance space. Here a blend of granite chips, stone paving and timber decking ensure variety.

3. PLANTING
A simple, low planting along the path to the seating area helps to offset the large expanses of paving in the garden and also brings greenery close to the most used part of the garden.

1. RETREAT

This small garden building is punching well above its weight in achieving a number of aims in its slender form: a focal point/eye-catcher and practical space in which to repose and enjoy the view across the garden back to the house. Its design is interesting, with a steeply swept roof line that is bordering on being too steep but that somehow manages to work, sitting as it does on slender pillars.

Elegant classic Gardens can often be as much about illusion as reality, using the horticultural equivalent of smoke and mirrors to cheat scale, give the illusion of space and detach the garden from whatever its setting is, however mundane, and place it in a more engaging context. This small town garden has aspirations of classical grandeur that could easily prove to be 'ideas above its station', but for the confidence with which those aspirations have been realised. The result is actually rather restrained and pretty, a calm and restful space.

2. HEDGING

The position and scale of the hedges in this garden creates a very definite garden room at the centre of the site, comprised almost entirely of lawn, whilst not compromising the views to and from the garden building or closing down the overall space.

3. LAWN

Though a lawn can be a liability in small gardens, damaging easily under footfall and proving tricky to maintain, here it is hard to envisage what else would work in a garden where the references to classical influences are subtle, but still important.

4. CLIPPED BOX

The simple device of repeated pots of clipped box creates a unifying presence through the garden, as well as introducing the suggestion of that quintessential classical garden feature, topiary.

5. STEPS

In a rectangular garden the obvious orientation for a flight of steps is at a right angle with the boundary. Here the steps are to one side and canted at an angle, which adds to the sense of a journey through the garden.

1. SEATING
Seating areas abound in this garden. The orientation of the different areas allows for the sun to be enjoyed, or avoided, whatever the time of day.

3. BOLD PLANTING
Architectural plants make a strong visual statement in this garden, including ferns, palms, olives and fastigiate junipers. The combination of plants adds to the Mediterranean flavour and provides year-round interest.

2. CLIPPED BOX
A pair of clipped box balls in oversized terracotta long tom containers act as sentinels or gate posts for the larger seating area, helping to divide the garden into particular areas or 'zones'.

Mediterranean style Bright, clean contemporary lines are mixed in this garden with a blend of strongly architectural plants and a high proportion of containerised plants, to create a garden that has the simplicity of modernist design in its hard landscaping but the eclecticism of less-formalised gardens in its planting, and a strong reference to the sunny courtyard gardens of the Mediterranean. The repeated use of seating areas in different locations – there are three in what is quite a small space – instantly create a journey from one space to another, the spaces as much decreed and delineated by the seating and tables as by any physical feature.

4. SOMEWHERE TO EAT The smaller of the two seating/dining areas has been located adjacent to the distinctive water feature to make best use of its cooling presence. There is a neat colour reference to the larger seating area: the colour of the table top matches that of the seats around the rectangular table.

Rooftop container garden The hidden green lungs of our cities, perched on building tops, rooftop gardens provide an important opportunity for many urban dwellers to connect with the green world. Because the soil on a rooftop is usually restricted to containers, and the exposure to sun and wind even more unrelenting than at ground level, maintaining moisture levels and preventing desiccation is a constant battle. This rooftop garden demonstrates just how much can be achieved in a space that would normally never see the greenery of plants.

1. SCREENING Vertical planting, in the form of containerised trees, helps screen not only surrounding lateral views but also overlooking views from several storeys up. These trees also help to provide much-needed shelter from buffeting winds.

2. SHELTERED SEATING The seating area in this garden has been very deliberately located in the lee of the adjoining building to take full advantage of any shelter it provides from the wind.

3. CONTAINER PLANTING Every plant in this garden has been grown in a pot, as there is no soil to plant into here. Clustering the containers together creates the sense of a planted border and allows you to try out a number of planting combinations – if you don't like one then simply move the pots around!

4. TIMBER DECKING The deck in this garden functions much as a typical grass lawn would; it is an open space which breaks up the overall composition and can be flexibly used. It's practical too, as timber decking is much lighter than a stone or concrete surface and so ideal for a rooftop.

Low-maintenance indulgence

This roughly south-facing garden in a small town in Wiltshire is typical of many rectangular gardens with timber fences forming the boundaries to each side. The owners, a couple who have owned the property for many years, have cultivated a serious interest in plants and gardens and, with the advent of retirement, now want to indulge themselves.

One serious challenge with the garden is the presence of two semi-mature trees, a lime (*Tilia cordata*) (N) and fastigiate hornbeam (*Carpinus betulus* 'Fastigiata') (I) both of which are subject to Tree Protection Orders (TPOs) from the local authority, prohibiting felling or heavy pruning without written permission. The consequent design incorporates both trees and celebrates their presence by removing garden elements that are compromised by large trees – stone paving that can become slippery during leaf fall, lawns that are impossible to keep looking good without huge investment of time and money, large ponds that can become clogged with leaves – and instead emphasises the benefits of having plants with such presence in the garden.

A: Steps
These steps lead from the first-floor living room into the garden. There is access from the ground floor too.

B: Outdoor dining/entertaining
The presence of the trees within this garden means that this area of hard paving near the house is the only open spot with decent sunlight through the day, making it suitable for turning into a garden room for entertaining and relaxing in the sun. At its centre is the only bit of natural stone in the garden, a bespoke feature made from ground and polished granite edged with rough-cut granite setts.

C: Bench seats
These built-in timber benches form permanent seating in the garden and are backed with fragrant plants, a simple planting comprising *Trachelospermum*

jasminoides, Lavandula 'Twickel Purple', and *Rosa* 'Rosarie de l'Hay'.

D: Pots
Framing the long view up the garden are a pair of extra-tall 'long tom' pots, planted with box *(Buxus sempervirens)* clipped into balls. To either side are dividing fences with scalloped ends that drop to meet the rim of the pots. Rather than solid fences these have large apertures between each horizontal slat, to allow as much light through as possible.

E: Deck path
By using cedar decking, a path has been made from one end of the garden to the other without the need for excavation, which could have seriously damaged the roots of the two feature trees. Cedar is an attractive, low-maintenance choice of timber for such a path, and laying sections of deck in blocks that alternate from

horizontal to vertical alignment creates additional interest.

F: Water features
Three zinc trough water features line the path, each equipped with a pump and filter to keep the water clear of weed. The reflective quality of water helps to enhance the light levels beneath the shade of the trees, and the relative shallowness of the troughs makes it easy to keep them clear of leaves.

G, H & K: Planted areas
These areas have been planted with shade- and semi-shade-tolerant plants including; *Anemone hupehensis, Geranium endressii, Convallaria majalis, Asplenium scolopendrium, Rodgersia podophylla, Pachyphragma macrophylla, Epimedium youngianum* and *Kirengeshoma palmata.*

I: Hornbeam tree

J: Storage
The very necessary, but not especially aesthetically pleasing, garden shed is here made into part of a dividing barrier that, along with a stub fence opposite, creates a third 'room' in the garden.

L: Planted area (*see page 166*)
Underneath the hornbeam tree is a planting scheme adapted to the conditions its canopy and roots create – shade and dry soil respectively.

M: Garden pavilion
This simple, timber pavilion is a tongue-in-cheek reference to a nearby stately home that the owners often visit. It forms the culmination of the garden and provides a seating spot to enjoy the views back into the garden.

N: Lime Tree (*Tilia cordata*)

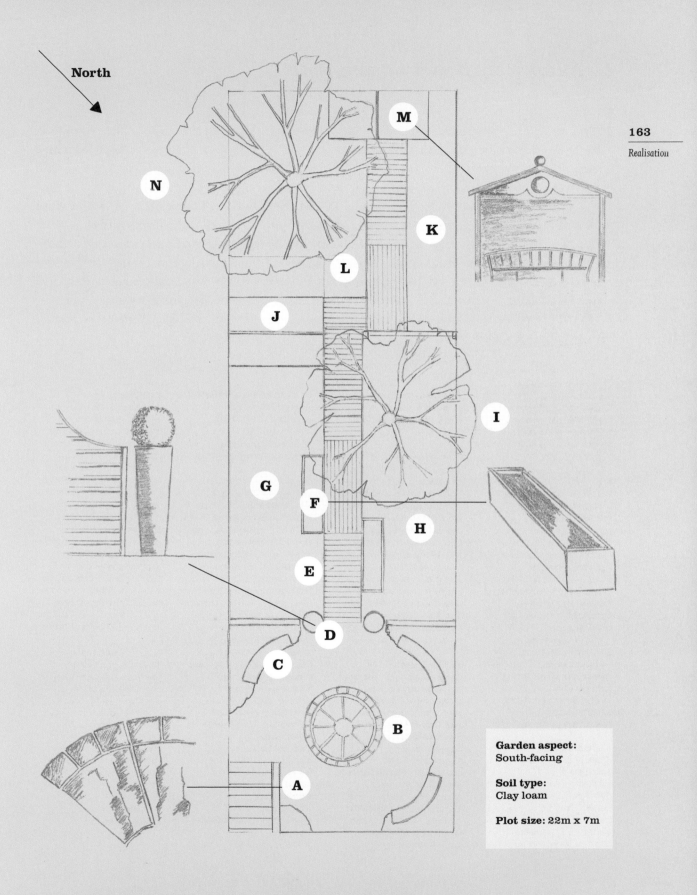

North

Garden aspect:
South-facing

Soil type:
Clay loam

Plot size: 22m x 7m

Making a difficult space work

This very small garden in west London provides several big challenges. Being north-facing, it is in shade until mid-afternoon, when the absence of any large structures on the western boundary enables the sun to cast its light across the garden until sunset. The presence of two large trees to the northern boundary means the soil at this end of the garden is quite dry and nutrient deficient, whilst the small size of the garden makes delivering the owners' wish list – which includes outdoor dining, covered seating, a barbecue and cooking area and somewhere for composting – very difficult indeed.

The resulting design is based on three interlocking circles of diminishing sizes, which enables the comfortable integration of features such as the barbecue and dining area to be orientated toward the late-afternoon sun. A shallow rill, a narrow water course that runs like a gully, creates movement and sound through the hard landscape. The planting features a lot of lush foliage plants, mostly permanent perennial plants but with some half-hardy plants such as banana and castor oil plant.

A: Paving
Double doors open onto this paved area of the garden which features container planting.

B & D: Planted areas
These areas have been planted with a minimalist semi-shade-tolerant planting of *Hakonechloa macra*, *Hosta sieboldii*, *Deschampsia cespitosa* 'Goldhange' and *Geranium phaeum album*.

C: Outdoor dining/ entertaining
In a small garden it can be tricky to accommodate any kind of storage for tables and chairs. Here a built-in bench and table, fashioned from heavy-gauge oak, have been constructed as permanent features, which can be softened and enlivened with colourful scatter cushions when in use.

The table and chairs are made from timber for continuity of materials.

E: Water rill
Essentially a shallow gully through which water flows, which can be easily stepped over, this rill has an additional reflective quality as the gully has been formed from stainless steel. It also adds a gentle background sound of running water to the garden, helping to mask the noise of nearby traffic.

F: Outdoor dining/ entertaining
This barbecue and food preparation area has been made using the same size oak as the built-in bench and dining table.

G: Snowy Mespilus
Paired Snowy Mespilus (*Amelanchier lamarckii*) help to 'pinch' the point at which the two main circles join, helping

to give the sense that the garden is divided into two distinct zones, without reducing the space in this cramped garden.

H: Covered curved seating
A covered, curved seating area, open at the sides, from where the rill emanates, creates a pleasant sensation as the water is right by the feet when sitting under the cover. As it is west-facing, the open front is exposed to the evening sun. A green sedum roof helps to minimise the visual impact of the structure, as well as maximising the greenery and potential wildlife habitats within the garden.

I: Sculpture
This feature sculpture acts as an 'eye-catcher' as it is located on the main vista through the garden.

J: Planted area
(*see page 167*)
A planting of full sun loving species emphasises the effectiveness of composing plants with varying forms to create a sense of movement.

K: Concealed composting
This composting and utility area has been tucked away behind the covered seating to minimise its visual impact.

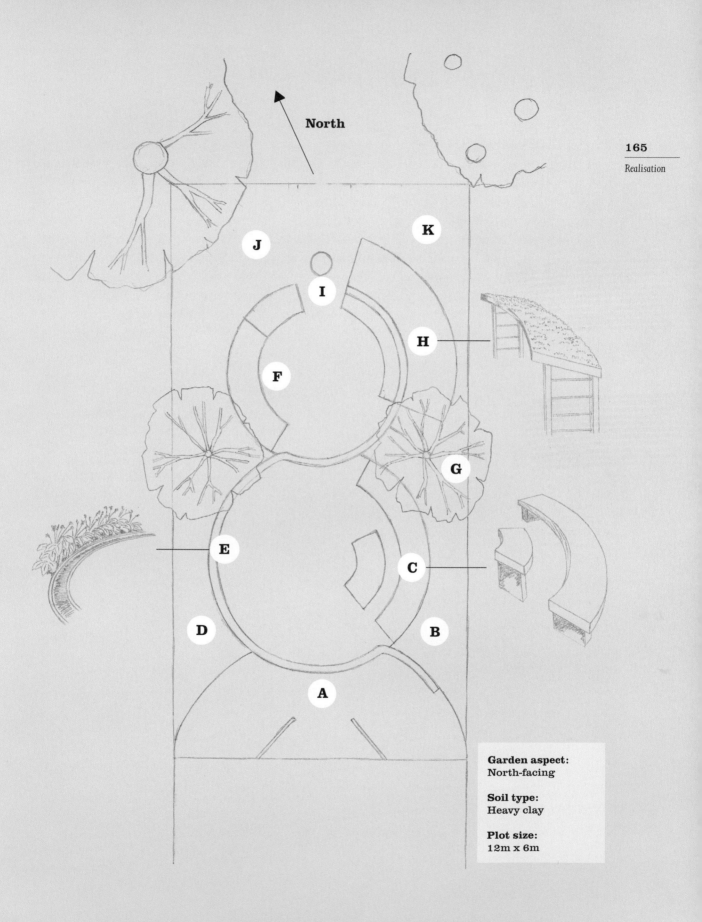

North

Garden aspect:
North-facing

Soil type:
Heavy clay

Plot size:
12m x 6m

Low-maintenance indulgence (p162)

Large, mature trees are wonderful to have in the garden, but they pose challenges if you want to try to grow anything underneath them as the combination of dry soil and shade creates challenging conditions, while the roots of the tree can be as impenetrable to dig around as concrete.

To improve the soil before planting, generous layers of grit – to improve drainage whilst enhancing moisture retention – as well as spent mushroom compost were applied to the surface over a period of six months, allowing weathering and soil-dwelling animals such as earthworms to help break down and absorb the compost into the soil. Plants were purchased small (nothing larger than a 1 litre pot) so that they didn't require vast amounts of watering. All the plants are adapted to shade, with the aim of the planting being to create an idealised woodland glade with the emphasis on the texture and form of foliage, sprinkled through with flowers. Bulbs are drifted throughout the planting, crossing over and through groups of plants to provide a more natural effect.

Planted area L

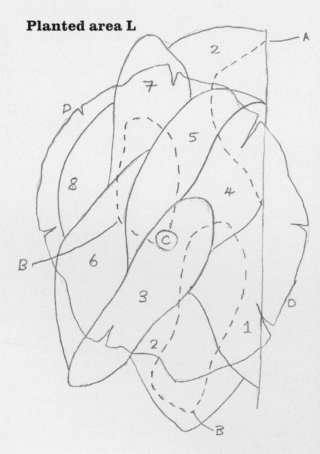

1. *Tellima grandiflora* Strong growing with coarse, mid-green leaves and plenty of foamy yellowy green flowers. Seeds itself around if the conditions are good for it to do so. 40cm x 30cm

2. *Brunnera macrophylla* 'Jack Frost' The leaves are splashed with pewter silver, lighting up dark shaded spots. Pale forget-me-not blue flowers. 60cm x 35cm

3. *Pulmonaria* 'Blue Ensign' Lovely, intense blue flowers early on in the season before the lime tree is in leaf. Looks lovely with spring bulbs. 25cm x 25cm

4. *Polystichum setiferum* 'Herrenhausen' One of the best ferns for dry shade, and adds great foliage interest and architectural strength. 1.2m x 50cm

5. *Vinca minor* 'Gertrude Jekyll' A tough, trouble-free ground-covering evergreen, very compact with pretty white flowers that is ideal for filling a space where little else grows. 10cm x indefinite

6. *Hosta* 'Big Daddy' Big, bold, blue-green leaves (28cm long). Suitable for sun or shade. 60cm x 1m

7. *Chaerophyllum hirsutum* 'Roseum' Adds an uncultivated, wild look to a planting. with finely cut, fern-like foliage topped with dusky-pink flowers. 60cm x 30cm

8. *Onoclea sensibilis* This lovely fern has very light-green fronds that emerge with a pinkish bronze tinge in spring and turn butter-yellow in autumn. 60cm x indefinite

A. *Narcissus* 'Hawera'
B. *Narcissus* 'Jetfire'
C. Existing Hornbeam (*Carpinus betulus* 'Fastigiata')
D. Tree canopy

Making a difficult space work (p164)

Though composing plants effectively can seem daunting, there are some compositional 'rules' that it pays to follow. This planting, viewed head on, demonstrates how to use a mixture of low-, mid- and tall-growing plants with varying forms to create a sense of movement that wouldn't exist if all the plants were the same or similar size, shape and form. The dotted line shows how the plants have been ordered according to their height hierarchy. As this part of the garden was the only one getting full sun, and the owners wanted minimal-maintenance input, the plants used are drought-tolerant and require only limited intervention to keep looking good. There is a subtle purple/bronze colour theme running throughout the planting, sometimes just a hint of colour, other times very boldly represented. There are also plenty of bulbs that love hot, dry conditions strewn throughout the planting, including *Sternbergia lutea*, *Colchicum autumnalis* and a variety of *Crocus*. To get the soil in good shape a 25cm layer of sharp grit was dug into the top 40cm of soil, along with a 30cm layer of spent mushroom compost.

Planted area J

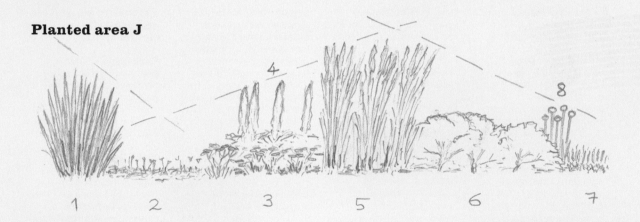

1. ***Phormium*** **'Bronze Baby'** Has very strong architectural merit, making it perfect for marking the end of a planted area, as here, with its bold, sword-like bronze leaves.
1.2m x 80cm

2. ***Eschscholzia californica*** This plant spreads readily by seed and will fill places that other plants cannot reach. Bright orange flowers, tough as old boots.
25cm x 15cm

3. ***Sedum telephium* subsp. *maximum* 'Matrona'** The flowers of this particular sedum are secondary to the foliage, which is a glossy, purple bronze, providing a colour link to the *Phormium*.
60cm x 30cm

4. ***Eremurus stenophyllus*** Adds a vertical element and a sense of drama, with vivid acid-yellow flowers in towering spikes.
1m x 60cm

5. ***Calamagrostis* x *acutiflora* 'Karl Foerster'** This grass acts like a punctuation mark in the planting, and provides long-term interest from May until December, with its purple flower heads.
1.8m x 60cm

6. ***Cistus argenteus* 'Peggy Sammons'** Smothered in purple-pink, papery flowers during summer. Contrasts in shape with the *Phormium*.
1m x 1.5m

7. ***Salvia* x *sylvestris* 'Tänzerin'** Hardy Salvia are some of my favourite plants, and this one is especially effective, with intense purple-blue flowers with a dash of red.
50cm x 30cm

8. ***Allium* 'Globemaster'** Adds another shape to the planting: the perfectly spherical, metallic purple flower heads, which last in the border as dried flowers for months.
80cm x 20cm

The family garden with a twist

This long, rectangular garden in south-east London is a good example of how a brief can sometimes change mid process. The owners, a young professional couple, discovered that they were going to become parents shortly after commissioning the design. So instead of the ultimate party garden, a garden with wider uses became the desired objective – somewhere to grow a few vegetables, a space for the baby to crawl and eventually toddle, and a place to entertain friends and dine outside too – after all, life doesn't stop when you have children!

The long, rectangular nature of the garden led to an early decision to shift the axis from up and down to across at an angle, immediately creating more of a sense of a journey through the garden and ensuring that elements of the space remained hidden unless explored. The same angle was applied to a number of features: a timber jetty, pergola, flower beds and a raised pool, to help enhance the cohesion in the garden.

A: Hard surface
Paved seating area for seating/outdoor dining.

B: 'Reversed' pergola
This is in effect two single-sided rows of posts that meet in the middle to form a single arch in the centre, with a further arch at the terminal end of the timber jetty on either side of which they are fixed. In a smaller garden where a full-sized pergola might seem oppressively dominant, this kind of structure brings the benefits of framed views into the garden and vertical presence, without overwhelming the space.

C: Timber jetty
Linking the paved dining/seating area with the rest of the garden via a timber jetty gives the initial journey into the garden a real sense of purpose, and also allows the garden to be viewed in a number of ways through various 'windows' formed by the pergola. Keeping the lawn side of the jetty open means that one can step off at any point, which reduces wear and tear that can occur if access is over a small patch of lawn.

D: Seating
Oak bench, made from a single rectangular beam of green (unseasoned) oak.

E: Lawn
A small, but essential lawn space for the children to crawl and toddle around in.

F: Artwork
One of the owners is an artist, so providing an outdoor space for interchangeable artwork was essential, and locating it at the end of the jetty gave it a sense of purpose as a focal point. It can also be glimpsed obliquely from the seating area and a number of other points in the garden.

G: Raised pool
This 3.5m x 1m x 0.45m pool brings the reflective, calming and aural qualities without any of the risk attached to water and small children. The 450mm raised sides are high enough to prevent a toddler from falling or climbing in, and can be augmented with a grille fitted across the surface of the water at a later date.

H: Barbecue and food preparation area

I: Paved area with additional seating

J: Raised beds
These raised beds have been created with the intention of growing a range of vegetables including courgettes, runner beans, spinach and potatoes.

K & M: Planted areas
These areas have been planted with semi-shade-tolerant plants including *Mileum effusum* 'Aureum', *Digitalis purpurea*, *Smyrnium perfoliatum*, *Pulmonaria* 'Opal', *Lilium martagon* var. *album*, *Heuchera* 'Persian Carpet', *Helleborus* x *hybridus*, *Euphorbia jacquemontii* and *Omphalodes cappadocica*.

**L: Planted area
(*see page 167*)**
Distinctive waterside planting creates a dramatic display in and around the raised pool (G).

N: Fruit trees
A pair of existing plum trees help to accentuate the angled design of the garden. Originally there were four small trees in the garden, which were thinned out to leave just these two.

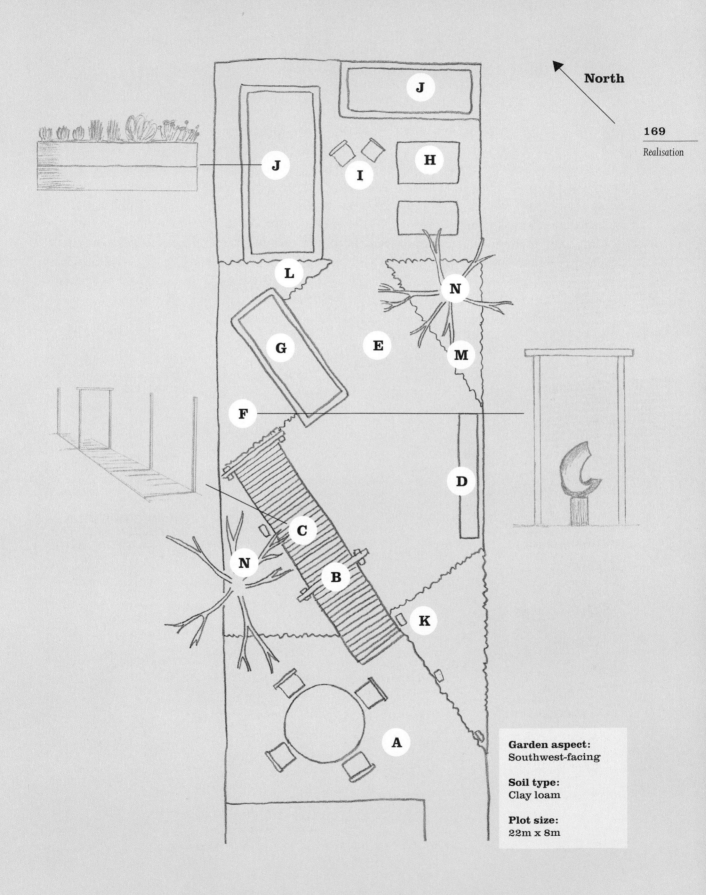

Garden aspect:
Southwest-facing

Soil type:
Clay loam

Plot size:
22m x 8m

Seaside gardens represent several interesting challenges. This garden on the south coast of England is east-facing, but the proximity of the sea – just one row of houses away – and a lack of other properties within 30m of the boundaries, ensure that it is as sunny as if it were facing due south. The soil in the area is quite poor: sandy, fast-draining and with few nutrients, which when added to the full sun and strong salty winds can lead to plants drying out and wilting rapidly – so appropriate plant selection is vital.

The garden had previously consisted of a large area of lawn with a rock garden and borders to the side, and the owner wanted to reduce the level of maintenance – especially the area of lawn – and increase the number of flowers. She also wanted to create the illusion of privacy by obscuring some of the overlooking windows of properties on the eastern boundary. The plan was very loosely based on the shape of a seahorse, the spine of the animal forming the shape of the path from the house to the garden shed.

A: Doors
Double doors lead from the second bedroom into the garden.

B: Kitchen window

C: Paving
A paved sandstone area features a large selection of containers planted with drought-tolerant plants.

D: Spiral paving detailing
An inset detail of square, polished granite pavers, which also form the edge of the main path is arranged in a spiral. This breaks up what would otherwise be a large expanse of paving and forms the notional 'tail' of the seahorse.

E: Curved pathway
Formed of over-fired, burnt stock pavers – a burnt stock means that the brick has been fired until the sand turns to glass, which as well as giving the brick distinctive black/purple patches also renders it non-slip as it becomes resistant to moss and algae growth – with an edge of polished granite pavers. The brick-red that is the primary colour in the burnt stock is also present in the sandstone paving flags in the main paved area, providing continuity of colour. The curving, looping path makes for a much more interesting journey, even if it is just to a shed!

F: Mini lawns
Although one of the main aims of the redesign was to get rid of the large lawn, two small panels of grass, easily cut with a lightweight rechargeable battery-powered mower, were included in the new design, to help set off the planted borders as well as to provide a space for the grandchildren to play on.

G: 'Amber Beauty' trees
Three *Prunus maackii* 'Amber Beauty' cut across the diagonal axis of the garden. Arranging the trees in this way helped to obscure some of the distant overlooking windows but also brought vertical height and much-needed shade into the heart of the garden, rather than banishing it to the fringes. 'Amber Beauty' is grown mainly for its attractive orange bark, which is especially striking in winter.

H: Planted area (*see page 173*)
The planting scheme here is full of colour and rich with different species.

I: Feature screening
A curved row of round, milled oak posts with clematis (in keeping with the garden's curved theme) partially obscure the shed – a better option than creating a flat-sided fence or trellis in front of the shed, which would only accentuate its presence.

J: Seating area
A bespoke, curving bench located in the dappled shade of one of the three *Prunus* trees.

K: Shed and compost area

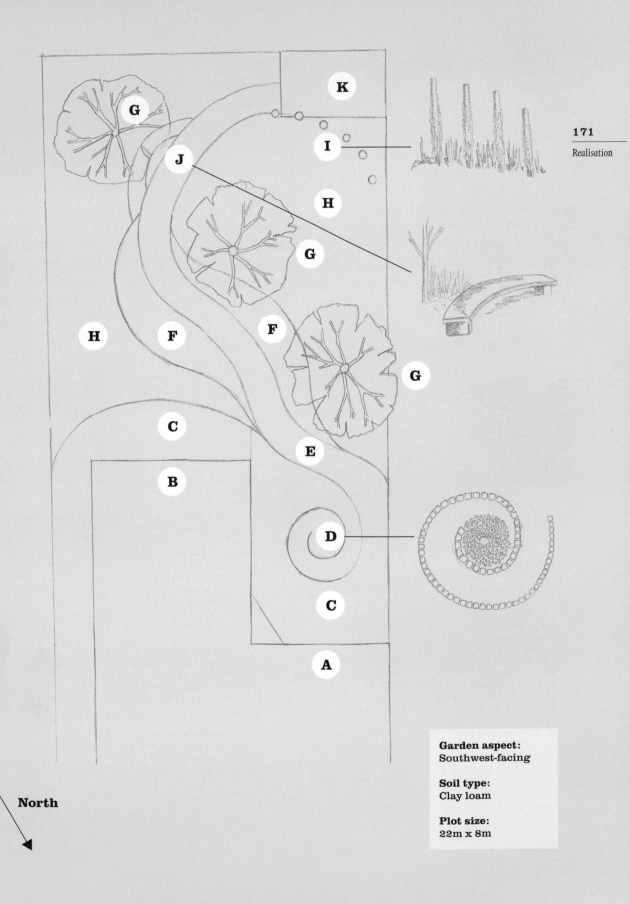

Garden aspect:
Southwest-facing

Soil type:
Clay loam

Plot size:
22m x 8m

North

The family garden with a twist (p168)

The rectangular raised pool, crafted from planed hardwood railway sleepers (*see area 'G' page 168*) forms the centrepiece of this planting area, counterbalancing the many foliage plants that surround it. The planting is in keeping with the semi-shaded, moist, waterside theme suggested by the pool, though in actuality the soil around it is no moister than anywhere else in the garden as the pool is an entirely self-contained feature raised above ground level, rather than a natural body of water with wet margins. The pool itself is also a planting opportunity, allowing for a range of plants – visually linked to the those that surround it – to be employed that simply cannot be grown elsewhere in the garden. Substantial architectural plants such as *Cyperus papyrus* make a real impact here, adding vertical presence to the planting and forming additional eye-catchers to be glimpsed through the 'windows' of the reversed pergola (*see area 'B' page 168*).

Planted area L

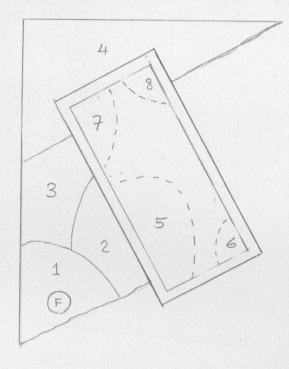

1. ***Deschampsia cespitosa* 'Goldtau'** This lovely cultivar illuminates semi-shade with golden flowers. 60cm x 60cm

2. ***Hosta* 'Halcyon'** Attractive, mid-sized blue-grey leaves that are gently tapered to a point. 50cm x 50cm

3. ***Ranunculus aconitifolius*** A very beautiful spring woodland plant, with white flowers and deeply cut leaves. 90cm x 60cm

4. ***Astilbe* 'Purpurlanze'** With its pretty purple flowers, this is one of the few Astilbe that tolerate drier soils. 1.2m x 70cm

5. ***Nymphaea pygmaea* 'Alba'** One of the smallest of all the water lilies (up to 25cm wide) and so suitable for a small pond such as this.

6. ***Iris ensata*** This water-loving iris is worth growing just for its sword-like foliage, let alone the purple flowers. 90cm x 30cm

7. ***Cyperus paperifera*** Cyperus papyrus the plant from which early paper was made, this is a great architectural water plant for sheltered, frost-free gardens. 1.8m x 60cm

8. ***Lythrum salicaria*** The lovely native purple loosestrife, a lovely sight when in bloom with its dusky-red-pink flowers. 1.2m x 50cm

Gardening by the seaside (p170)

The owner of the garden wanted lots of flowers in her garden, but the seaside location and relatively poor soil – it's fast draining and doesn't hold on to nutrients very well – meant careful plant selection was essential, good soil preparation vital, and the application of weed-suppressing and moisture-retaining mulch a time- and plant-saving boon. The soil was improved before planting with a 40cm layer of green waste compost from the local council waste-processing facility.

The overall design theme of the garden, a series of curves based around the main sweeping path and bisected by three prunus tree that strike across the garden, led naturally to a series of interlocking drifts of plants that followed the same flow as the path, creating a wave-like effect. Fragrant lavender was planted near the edge of the path and the seating area and a sweeping line of feature *Stipa gigantea* 'Gold Fontaine' planted to form a counter-curve to the main path. The result is a modernist, naturalistic update on the old-fashioned cottage garden.

Planted area H

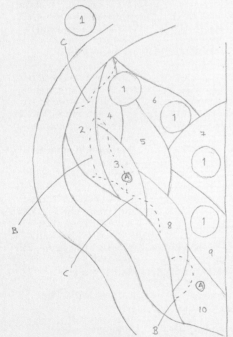

3. *Euphorbia amygdaloides* 'Purpurea' A great foliage interest plant, with dark-purple leaves topped by acid-yellow flowers.
50cm x 40cm

4. *Erysimum* 'Bowles' Mauve' This beautiful plant flowers so freely, that, after three or four years, it has flowered itself to death. But it is worth every moment.
75cm x 60cm

5. *Eryngium x zabelii* 'Jos Eijking' A relatively new cultivar with steely silver foliage and intense metallic-blue flowers, this is a perfect seaside plant and incredibly tough and drought-tolerant.
75cm x 50cm

6. *Helenium* 'Waldtraut' Upright and sturdy, this border stalwart flowers from midsummer into autumn, producing attractive golden-brown flowers that are a superb foil to steely eryngium.
100cm x 80cm

7. *Knautia macedonica* Tough and beautiful, with deep burgundy-coloured flowers that are much loved by bees and butterflies and, when turned to seed, finches.
1m x 50cm

8. *Salvia x sylvestris* 'Blauhügel' A compact hardy salvia that bears plenty of pretty purple-blue flowers over a long period through summer.
45cm x 45cm

9. *Persicaria amplexicaulis* 'Firetail' Long-flowering, from June until October, with tall spires of bright red flowers over attractive, robust foliage.
80cm x 60cm

10. *Nassella trichotoma* An extraordinary-looking grass, resembling the fibre-optic table ornaments popular in the 1970s.
50cm x 50cm

A. *Prunus maackii* 'Amber Beauty'
B. *Nigella damascena*
C. *Eschscholzia californica*

1. *Stipa gigantea* 'Gold Fontaene' Structural plants, with oat-like flowers on thin stems. Their see-through nature means that, despite their height, they can be planted near to the front of a border.
2m x 1.3m

2. *Lavendula* 'Vera' Taller than many of the more popular compact lavender, and with an attractive, loose habit that is particularly suitable in a cottage garden themed planting.
60cm x 40cm

Outdoor entertaining

This small south-facing garden in south London benefits from full sun for most of the day, but a slope from the house to the boundary fence make it hard to accommodate the outdoor dining and entertaining spaces that the owners, a young professional couple, want to include. In order to make the garden as useable as possible it has been reconceived as two level areas with a 1m high terrace between them, creating equal-sized zones for the garden's various features – a well-proportioned space for table and chairs, fragrant planting and a large pool. Detailing is vital in a garden of this size, and the pool offers the opportunity to mix high-quality diamond-cut sandstone (with a very smooth finish) with a cedar timber deck.

Whilst the owners very much want to include plants, they have concerns over the amount of time they would need to spend maintaining the garden and worry that an overly complex planting scheme would be beyond their abilities to look after. All planting within this garden has therefore to be as easy to care for as possible.

A: Water feature
In a small space it can be tempting to scale down the size of any planned garden features, but sometimes this can only serve to make the space seem even smaller and fussier. This rectangular pool, surrounded by a cedar timber deck, not only serves to cool down the top terrace of the garden (which, as it is south-facing and sheltered, could otherwise become uncomfortably warm) but also helps to create an illusion of greater space through the reflection of the sun and sky. Beneath the deck is a soakaway system that absorbs and slowly releases all the water run-off from the garden, which helps to reduce the flow of flood water into local water courses, and an underground water tank to take water from the house roof for irrigation.

B: Seating
This seating area for outdoor dining is surfaced with resin-bonded gravel, a stable, sealed aggregate that doesn't move or 'pick up' under foot.

C: Outdoor dining/entertaining
This large circular table is made from the same type of timber – cedar – as the timber deck and bench (I) to give continuity across the various timber elements.

D & K: Planted areas
Simple planting consisting of Lavender (*Lavendula* 'Hidcote') and clipped box pyramids. During summer the fragrance from the lavender pervades the entire top terrace, whilst the box pyramids provide structure, form and year-round presence. In spring the beds are enlivened with large drifts of the white daffodil *Narcissus* 'Thalia'.

E: Terrace wall and picture frame
A 1m high wall constructed from the same stone as the pool edge – diamond-cut sandstone – this time cut as blocks. Although comparatively expensive, using such high-quality materials sparingly ensures their impact is maximised. To the west of the garden a simple 'picture frame' of timber helps to subdivide the dining space and create windows onto the planting around the Magnolia.

F: Steps
These steps are made from the same diamond-cut sandstone as used in the terrace and pool edge.

G: Pleached hornbeam
An aerial hedge of hornbeam that rises above the 1.2m fence on the eastern boundary to a height of 2.3m and provides greater privacy from neighbours without becoming an oppressive nuisance.

H: Lawn
Small lawns can be a nightmare to look after, because of the level of wear and tear over a small area, but the owners were insistent and it provides an additional area for occasional chairs.

I: Seating
This timber bench has been placed next to *Sarcococca confusa*, a highly fragrant, shade-tolerant (this bed is north-facing and in almost complete shade) evergreen shrub that flowers in winter, when it will fill the garden with perfume. In a hot, sunny garden a shaded bench can provide a very welcome break from the heat.

J: Planted area
(*see page 178*)

L: Back door

M: Window

Garden aspect:
South-facing

Soil type:
Heavy clay

Plot size:
10m x 11m

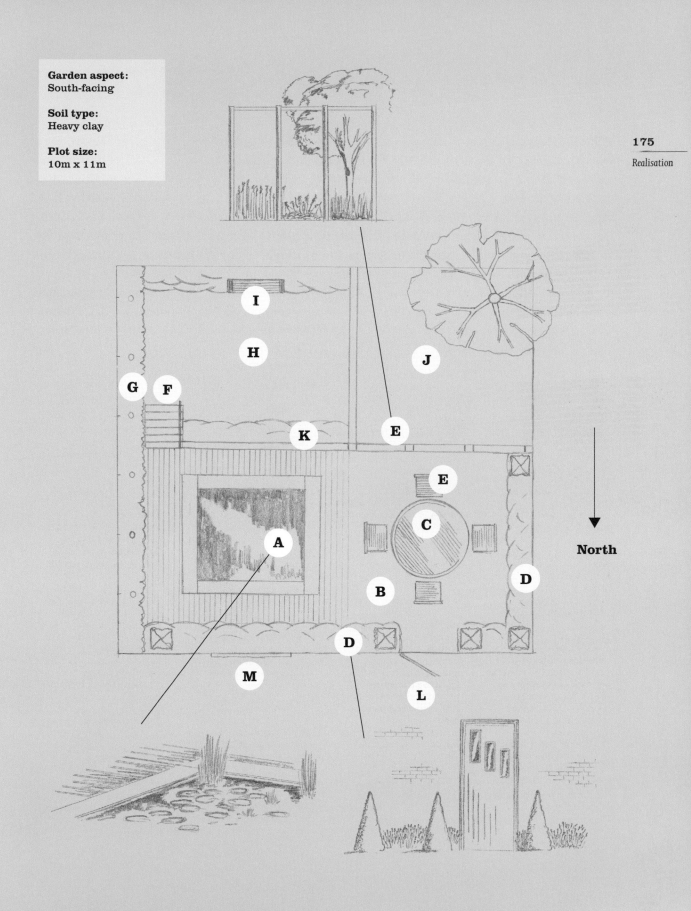

North

The unconventional front garden

Sometimes the only available, or suitable, space to make a garden is a 'non-traditional' one. This garden, located on a comparatively quite side street in Yorkshire includes many of the features associated with a garden space – seating area, pool, planting – but in this case they are in the front garden, rather than the rear. The reasons for this are twofold; the rear garden of this property is roughly east-facing and rather cool and shaded, plus the owners, a couple with two young children, have dedicated the small rear garden space to their youngsters and creating as many play opportunities as possible.

The front garden, however, offered easier growing conditions – west-facing – and enough space to make a viable ornamental garden that the whole family can enjoy, including an outdoor dining area, herb- and salad-growing space and ornamental pool. The owners have a very limited budget, so every effort has been made to make materials and features look as good as possible for the minimum outlay.

A: Yew trees
A pair of fastigiate yew trees, *Taxus baccata* 'Fastigiata' form offset markers to the garden gate and the terminal point of the first section of garden path. Chopping the path to the front door into two straight sections creates a greater sense of journey without making it impossible to negotiate – paths need to be practical, as well as aesthetically alluring. Repeating two plants with strong structural presence creates surprise and expands the vertical plane in a small space.

B: Planted area
(see page 179)
This area of the garden has been developed into a simple potager – a hardworking kitchen garden with beautiful, ornamental displays.

C: Fencing
Fences are rarely things of great beauty, but are often necessary where it is impossible to accommodate a more environmentally and aesthetically pleasing boundary feature such as a native hedge. A 'hit and miss' boundary fence creates a pleasing, permeable barrier and is achieved by removing every other, or every other two, posts, or a combination thereof.

D: Offset pathway
Rather than using expensive paving materials, the paths in this garden have been made using a sub-base of recycled crushed concrete topped with rolled granite chips. To give them a little extra quality, and to give a little extra visual interest, the paths have been edged with a granite sett.

E: Decking
This oak timber decking has been made from new untreated oak railway sleepers cut in half along their length – a cost-effective way of doubling the area of coverage from the same amount of materials. The decking is used around the main seating area but also near the front door to provide continuity of materials.

F & H: Planted areas
Informal planting of cottage garden favourites and other mixed perennials including *Astrantia* 'Hadspen Blood', *Dicentra spectabilis alba*, *Rosa glauca*, *Rosmarinus officianalis*, *Geranium* x *magnificum*, *Crocosmia* 'Lucifer', *Penstemon* 'Andenken an Friedrich Hahn', *Clematis recta*, *Campanula lactiflora* 'Sparkes' Variety', *Veronicastrum* 'Fascination', *Thalictrum* 'Elin' and *Cotinus* 'Grace'.

G: Water features
The two pools of water here appear as though they are a single water feature, crossed with a bridge, while in fact there is a solid path between them. The two pools are linked by an underground pipe so that just one filtration system is required, and a metal grate has been installed 1 cm below the water surface to ensure the children are safe from falling in the water.

I: Rowan tree
Pre-existing Rowan tree (*Sorbus* 'Joseph Rock')

J: Yew hedge
Yew (*Taxus baccata*) hedge to 1.6m

K: Outdoor dining/entertaining
Made from the same untreated oak sleepers as the deck, this outdoor dining table has a built-in herb and salad planter in the centre of the table – in effect a large timber box, lined with a waterproof membrane and drilled with drainage holes – that drops into the table. The perfect way to combine outdoor dining and growing, in this case augmented by containers with vegetables growing around the table.

L: Dining room window

M: Hall window

N: Front door

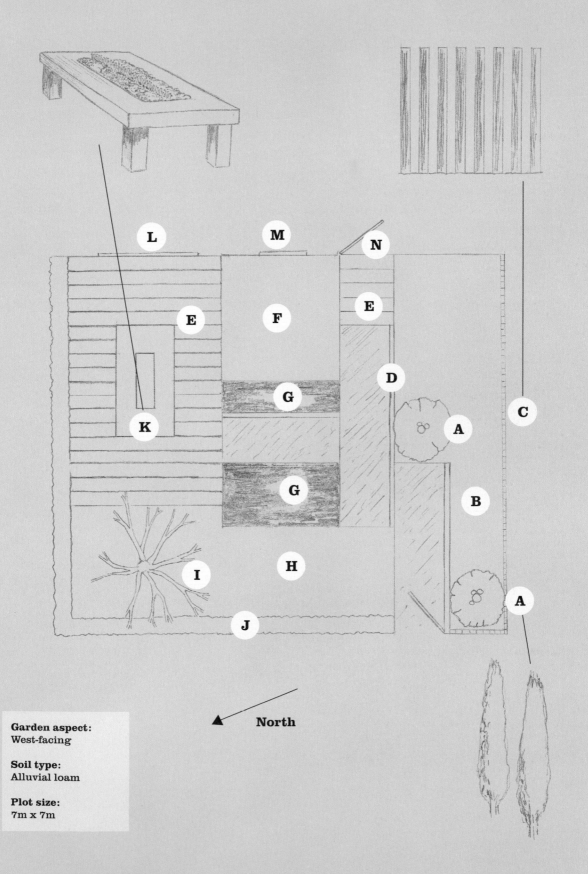

Garden aspect:
West-facing

Soil type:
Alluvial loam

Plot size:
7m x 7m

North

Outdoor entertaining (p174)

The owners of this garden wanted their limited area for mixed planting to be as texturally interesting, and colourful, as possible. The conditions – part sun, part shade – mean that plant selection is varied across the planted area with appropriate plants to suit. Rather than organising the plants into large drifts, this planting has a slightly looser arrangement and is closer to a matrix planting – where plants drift in and out of each other's space, as if they have self-seeded and mingled together. The effect has echoes of the way plants grow in the wild, whilst still being controlled and enabling plants to be deliberately positioned to maximise their aesthetic impact.

The clay soil and partial shade in this part of the garden was countered by the digging in of 25cm of sharp grit, 20cm of composted bark and 20cm of green waste manure from the local council into the top 40cm of soil. In order not to damage the tree roots, the material was applied to the top of the soil around the tree, in layers and over a period of six months, to allow it to break down into the soil.

Planted area J

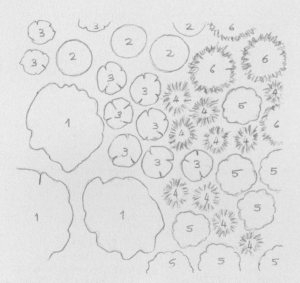

1. *Rosa* 'Complicata'
A lovely, old-fashioned rose with highly fragrant flowers that fill the garden with scent when in bloom during summer. It's also tough, and quite happy growing in clay-based soils – as are most roses.
1.8m x 1.8m

2. *Miscanthus yakushimensis* 'Little Kitten' More compact than the majority of *miscanthus*, with fine, light-green leaves marked with a creamy white central 'rib'. This ornamental grass bears silvery flowers from late summer.
70cm x 80cm

3. *Gillenia trifoliata* An under-used perennial with pretty, starry white flowers from early summer and great autumn foliage colour.
90cm x 50cm

4. *Stipa tenuissima* The hair grass is an irresistible textural treat, and a great plant for creating a sense of almost watery movement through a planting scheme. Best grown from seed, which it produces prodigiously.
60cm x 30cm

5. *Galega orientalis* Has a lovely, slightly wild look to it and copes with sun and partial shade, producing violet-blue flowers in spring and summer. It can spread a bit if the conditions are right, which may need managing.
1.2m x 60cm

6. *Spiraea japonica* 'Gold Flame' Brings a splash of foliage colour to a semi-shaded spot, producing bronze-red foliage in spring that then turns golden yellow before finally becoming green, at which point it produces dark-pink flowers.
75cm x 75cm

The unconventional front garden (p176)

Along with areas of flowering and foliage plants, the front garden offered the perfect space to grow vegetables and herbs in a 'potager' style – growing small amounts of edible plants mixed with flowering plants. Growing your own food is great fun, and there are environmental benefits in a reduced carbon footprint, along with the health benefits that come from knowing exactly where your food has come from and what has gone into making it grow. And for children there are wonderful educational opportunities – there is nothing quite like seeing a plant grow from seed to maturity, and then eating it!

But in a small space it's vital to grow the crops that benefit the most from being harvested fresh or that have a premium attached to them. So rows of potatoes and cabbages are out, replaced by tasty herbs, hard-to-find vegetables and expensive crops like asparagus. These are mixed with flowering plants that act as companion plants by either drawing pests away from the crop or masking the smell of vegetables so that pests cannot locate them. The alluvial loam in the garden was in good condition but benefitted from the addition of well-rotted manure, dug into the top 50cm of soil

Planted area B

1. *Rosa* 'Gertrude Jekyll' One of the most fragrant of the new English roses. Here it's grown mainly for its scent and beauty although aphids will be attracted to it and can be dealt with using an organic spray or natural predators.
1.3m x 1.3m

2. Purple sprouting broccoli A high-value crop that has a relatively short shelf life, so is well worth growing even if only a few plants. It will crop throughout late winter and early spring, a lean time for home-grown produce.

3. Swiss chard Another winter-cropping plant. The variety 'Bright Lights' is particularly colourful.

4. *Delphinium* 'Black Knight' This imposing border favourite is highly attractive to slugs and snails – helping to draw them away from the veg.
1.6m x 70cm

5. Jerusalem artichoke A tasty, expensive crop and a seriously impressive architectural plant. The flowers are loved by bees.

6. Asparagus Although it takes three seasons from planting before harvesting can commence, this high-value crop is well worth the effort.

7. Garlic Whilst not very expensive, the range of garlic varieties to grow is far wider than can be bought in the shops. The giant elephant garlic is great for roasting.

8. Little Gem lettuce Easy to grow and fast to crop, Little Gems can be grown to maturity in a matter of weeks.

9. Lollo rosso An easy-to-grow salad leaf with a distinctive taste and a great colour contrast to green lettuce.

10. *Allium schoenoprasum* (chives) Lovely to have at hand for garnishing salads, especially potato salad. Its flowers are edible too.

11. *Nasturtium* The peppery leaves are a tasty treat in salads, but this is also a sacrificial plant as aphids are drawn to it in preference to the rest.

12. *Molinia caerulea* subsp. *arundinacea* 'Transparent' A lovely ornamental grass that has height and presence without bulk. Good for cutting but also provides a habitat for a variety of beneficial insects.
1.8m x 60cm

The hybrid garden

With many small domestic gardens the architectural integrity of the house is secondary to creating a garden that works practically and aesthetically. In this case however, the house – a 1960s modernist property designed by the architectural practice SPAN as part of a development in Kent – demands a particular approach, respecting the very strong architectural features of the property, the rear, garden elevation of which is based around a series of cube-like bays. The owners, a professional couple, were very clear about what they wanted – simple structural planting but also lots of flowers and informality – which at times conflicted with an ultra-minimal, modernist garden. The result is something of a hybrid, with areas of wild meadow, planted bays of colour drawn in size and shape directly from the staggered cube bays of the house, and structural hedges to create a series of crisp horizontal lines through the garden.

The rear elevation of this detached house faces almost due north, but the amount of space and absence of neighbouring structures means that there is plenty of sunshine in the main planting areas.

A: Rear elevation of house

B: Decking
Large cedar deck to accommodate dining and sitting out.

C: Hot tub
This hot tub has been built flush with the surrounding deck.

D: Paving
Paved area with four rectangular Portland stone paving flags. These paving flags link aesthetically to a roof terrace on the first floor of the building which is entirely paved with Portland stone. High-quality natural stone can be a great aesthetic asset but is often expensive; however, even a small amount of high-quality stone can make an impact in a garden, if used in a high-profile position and installed with skill.

E: Seating
This Portland stone bench, made from the same stone as above, is inset into a beech (*Fagus sylvatica*) hedge which is in turn backed by a white painted brick wall. The result is a very cool, sleek seating area with views back into the garden and house that also acts as a focal point from the other end of the garden.

F: Planted area (see page 184)

G: Beech hedge
A beech hedge (*Fagus sylvatica*) in three sections of varying lengths echoes the cubed rear section of the house. Each bay that is created by the hedges houses a section of the perennial planting (F). The hedges are also cut at three diminishing heights (2m, 1.7m, 1.4m), to create a strong horizontal architectural form in the garden.

H: Orchard and wildflower meadow
This rectangular section of the garden used to house a lean-to car port and tarmac hard standing for parking. This was ripped up and replaced with a mini orchard and wildflower meadow, which creates a very striking contrast to the sleek, white painted minimalist architecture of the house. The five trees are a mixture of apple, pear and plum and the wildflower meadow was seeded with seed harvested from local meadows. The combination of long grass and flowers beneath old orchard trees harks back to a time when these were common sights in the area of Kent where the house is located.

I: Mown grass pathway
A simple mown grass path meanders through the orchard and wildflower meadow.

J: Seating
This Portland stone bench is identical to the one inset into the beech hedge on the other side of the garden. Using the same feature twice but in a different context creates an interesting dynamic between continuity of materials and contrast of setting.

K: Sculptures
Two sculptures, the work of the same artist and bought as a pair, stand in opposing corners of the orchard meadow. The owners purchased the works from an art college graduation show, an excellent way to buy new art at reasonable prices and support up-and-coming artists.

L: Doors
Double French doors lead out into the garden.

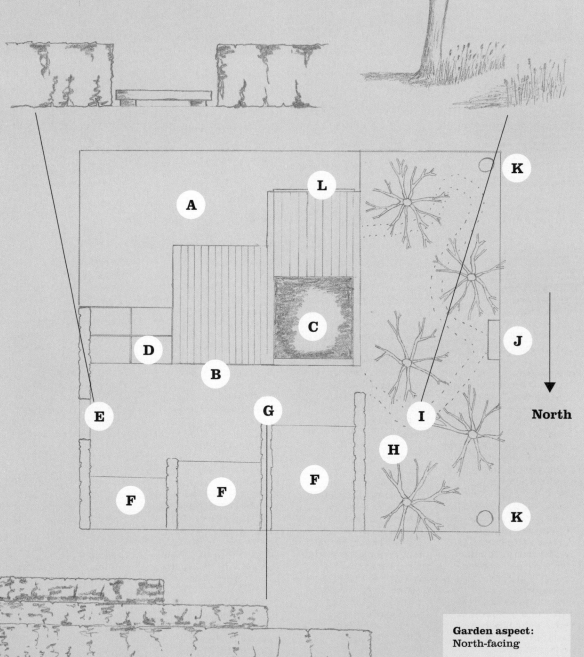

Garden aspect:
North-facing

Soil type:
Sandy loam

Plot size:
30m x 30m

North

The surprising space

This garden on the Channel Island of Guernsey is a hundred metres or so from the sea and protected from the worst of the weather, to an extent, by 3m high walls that wrap around it. As well as facing the typical seaside challenges of high light levels, salt winds and dry, hot conditions, there's an added complication in that the area which is now garden used to be where the owners' cars were parked, and so consisted of tarmac rather than soil. The garden is also a slightly odd shape, with one boundary wall cutting across the garden at an angle.

To manage the unusual shape and lack of soil, the garden is based around interlocking circles of decked hard standing, edged with low raised walls that enable the imported topsoil (after removing the tarmac there was no soil to replace it with) to be built up by 300mm, giving not just a greater depth of soil to plant into but also a sense, at least when the plants are established, that the seating areas are slightly sunken.

A: Conservatory

B: Water feature
This raised, curved water feature discharges water over a low (450mm) lip into a splash area below, creating a steady, calming and cooling sound – perfect in such a hot, sunny garden.

C: Fire pit
This fire pit turns the sunny seating area into a warm evening retreat, ideal for a drink or meal as the sun sets.

D: Built-in seating

E: Decking
In a very sunny garden a timber deck, such as this oak one, has a slight advantage over stone as it doesn't absorb quite as much heat, so is less likely to become uncomfortably hot to walk on after several hours of exposure to full sun.

F: Planted barrier
Double-skinned hollow wall, 500mm high, built from rendered blocks,

that have been filled with topsoil and planted with aromatic drought-tolerant plants including lavender, rosemary, *Artemesia*, *Nepeta* and thyme. A planted hollow wall offers the opportunity to create a barrier with a lower visual impact than a solid wall, and that maximises the space available for plants.

G: Tree grove
Grove of *Elaeagnus* 'Quicksilver', a silver-leaved, highly fragrant drought- and wind-tolerant large shrub/small tree. Planted here they help to break up the outline of the garage (J) and provide a degree of shelter from westerly wind.

H: Trained trees
Two roof-trained *Elaeagnus multiflora* provide form, structure and cast shade in the second seating area, creating a cooler space for sitting in than the sun drenched oak deck.

I: Screening
A row of clipped evergreen holm oak, *Quercus ilex*, provide an additional screen against seas winds, of which this plant is highly tolerant, and also helps to soften the appearance of the 3m tall wall.

J: Garage

K: Planted area
(*see page 185*)

L, M & N: Planted areas
These beds have been planted with sun-loving plants including *Ballota pseudodictamnus*, *Eryngium x oliverianum*, *Artemesia arborescens*, *Ozothamnus rosmarinifolius*, *Stipa gigantea*, *Corokia virgata*, *Helianthemum* 'Henfield Brilliant', *Ceanothus* 'Concha', *Sternbergia lutea*, *Helichrysum petiolare*, *Diascia rigescens*, *Verbena rigida*, *Arum creticum*.

O: Box hedging
Clipped box (*Buxus sempervirens*) balls provide structure and repetition around the edge of the main seating area and also, through their shape, reference the interlocking circles that are the theme of the garden.

North

Garden aspect:
South-facing

Soil type:
Loam

Plot size:
18m x 24m

The hybrid garden (p180)

The rectangular planting bays in this garden are hemmed in by hedges and so therefore only readily viewed 'head on'. Consequently the hierarchy of plants, organised by height from front to back as well as considerations of colour, texture and form, is even more important to get right than in a planting where plants can be viewed from several sides. However, structuring everything evenly by height from front to back can appear a little too uniform, and it's good to throw in one or two taller plants nearer the front, providing they aren't too solid-looking but instead have a wafting, translucent feel.

Given that the house is such a strong architectural presence, and the ethos of the garden is one of low-environmental impact, the choice of plants needed to be naturalistic in appearance and suitable for the sandy soil too. It was also important to recognise the aesthetic established by the meadow and orchard, so that when looking across the borders toward the meadow the view was a gradation of planted to natural, rather than a jolting sudden shift. The colour theme in this bay is dusky pinks and reds, with late summer and autumn the principal flowering time.

The sandy soil was improved with well-rotted, chopped farmyard manure dug into the top 30cm, and then mulched with spent mushroom compost.

Planted area F

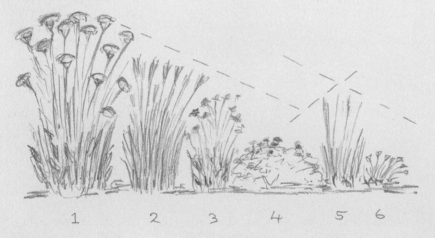

1. *Eupatorium purpureum*
A statuesque border perennial with a suitably wild look, being a native to damp meadows and woodland edges in North America. It has large, dusky-pink flowers that are adored by bees, butterflies and moths.
2m x 80cm

2. *Miscanthus sinensis* 'Ferner Osten'
Sits perfectly in front of the *Eupatorium* and references its colour with dark-red inflorescences in autumn that fade to a light silver grey by winter. It also has fabulous autumn foliage colour.
1.8m x 70cm

3. *Echinacea purpurea* 'Magnus' Has especially big flowers, with a dark bristly central boss to each one, the rest of the flower dusky purple-pink.
1.2m x 60cm

4. *Geranium psilostemon* A great all-rounder with vivid magenta flowers in summer, each one with a conspicuous dark central 'eye'. During autumn this has some of the best foliage colour of all perennials, turning red, orange and deep burgundy.
1m x 1m

5. *Molinia caerulea* subsp. *caerulea* 'Edith Dudzsus' Dropping this *molinia* into the composition at this point disrupts the continuous flow of diminishing height, making it a lot more interesting as a result. The see-through nature of this grass means that it doesn't obscure the plants behind it.
1.5m x 40cm

6. *Hemerocallis* 'Little Wine Cup' This lovely, low-growing day lily has dark-burgundy flowers in summer and decent foliage that turns butter-yellow in autumn.
30cm x 40cm

The surprising space (p182)

This part of the garden is baked by the sun and is incredibly hot, the heat amplified by the surrounding house and walls which 'bounce' light and warmth back into the garden. Consequently the only plants that can really thrive in such conditions are those on the more extreme edge of sun and drought adaptation. Fortunately the comparative absence of frost and cold winters on the Channel Islands means that exotic plants thrive here.

Stylistically the planting is best described as a xeroscape – a comparatively sparse planting of strongly architectural drought-proof plants along with flowering annuals and bulbs. The trick to making such a planting work aesthetically is to ensure there is space around the plants to allow the architectural presence of agave and echium to come through. Plant too many other plants around them and they lose their impact, becoming cast members rather than the stars of the show.

The soil in the garden needed no improvement to grow these sun-loving specialists, but a mulch comprised of pebbles of varying sizes from 5mm to 30mm, with a few larger paddle stones added in, helps to seal in moisture, keep down weeds and give a suitable rocky look to the garden, whilst also referencing the nearby seaside.

Planted area K

1. *Agave americana* Eventually becomes a beast of a plant, it is monocarpic – meaning it dies after flowering. A hugely impressive structural plant with blue-green, leathery leaves tipped with sharp spikes.
2m x 3m

2. *Echinops bannaticus* 'Taplow Blue' This pollen- and nectar-rich plant is known as the globe thistle, which describes its steely blue flowers well. It's suitable for any sunny spot but incredibly tolerant of really dry conditions, hence its inclusion here.
1m x 60cm

3. *Echium pininana* Another mighty beast that can reach as high as 4m, but more often is rather shorter. Smothered in blue flowers, loved by insects, a complete show off of a plant that impresses on every level and is completely drought-proof.
4m x 90cm

4. *Erodium x variabile* 'Ken Aslet' This low-growing sub-alpine plant thrives in hot conditions and well-drained soil. Here it forms a carpet of dusky pink between the major structural plants, reminiscent, if only on a tiny scale, of the incredible flush of wildflowers experienced in areas such as the Veldt in South Africa after the spring rains have fallen.
8cm x 30cm

5. *Leptospermum scoparium* 'Red Damask' The stems and foliage on this shrub are so fine and wiry that when it is in flower it seems to be a mass of dark-red blooms and nothing else.
2m x 2m

6. *Aloe striatula* Has thick, fleshy leaves rather like agave, and although on a smaller scale it is just as architecturally powerful, especially when producing its orange-yellow, waxy, nectar-rich flowers that resemble those of a red hot poker plant.
1m x 1.4m

'The first parts of the garden in Devon developed by Keith and Ros Wiley are now four years old and maturing into their full potential. A garden rarely looks beautiful by accident; behind the beauty is the planning, dreaming and scheming before the eventual act of realisation begins – an act that never stops as long as the garden lives. For the owners of the six gardens featured in *Landscape Man* and for all those who embark on the wonderful, life affirming process that is making a garden, aspiring to beauty will always be the aim, but the enjoyment of the journey is the real pleasure'.

Index

Index

Acknowledgements

Putting together a book of this nature is very much a team effort, and although my name appears on the front it is the work of many hands. Jane O'Shea, Simon Davis, David Rowley, Samantha Rolfe and Helen Lewis have contributed some of the most important of the many hands at Quadrille Publishing, and those I haven't mentioned I thank too; it has been a joy to work with such a creative team. My book agent Julian Alexander at LAW helped to craft the initial thoughts for the book, held my hand when needed, and introduced me to Quadrille and vice versa. *Landscape Man* is the brainchild of John Silver and Simon Bisset at Red House TV, with whom it has been my great privilege and honour to work for the last 10 months. Simon also took many of the beautiful photographs that grace these pages and has been a travelling companion *par excellence*. The Red House team, who have been like a second family throughout our time together, have made filming the series such a great experience; Nicks Bullard, Matt Cox, Ed St Giles, Lotta Hellzen, Matt Lees, Caroline McCool, Louisa MacInnes and Geri Sweeney. Thanks too to our wonderful contributors for allowing access to their gardens, and their dreams, and the superb camera and sound crews who captured the action, in particular Tony Etwell, Cliff Evans, Daniel Spencer and Mike Stephenson. Finally my warm thanks to Walter Iuzzolino at Channel 4 and my TV agent, Laura Hill at Independent, and to J Barbour and Sons Ltd for being so generous. This book is dedicated to my wonderfully supportive and patient wife, Jane, and our twin babies Amelie and Dylan, who came along just about halfway through the writing of the book and have put everything in perspective.

Picture credits

10-11© Simon Bisset; 15 Liz Eddison/The Garden Collection, design: Chris Beardshaw, RHS Chelsea 2007; 16 Elizabeth Balmforth; 17 Clive Nichols/Clare Matthews; 18 Steven Wooster/The Garden Collection, design: Laara Copley-Smith; 19 above Marcus Harpur, design: Justin Greer, London; 19 below www.modulargarden.com, tel: 020 76190100; 21 www.modulargarden.com, tel: 020 76190100; 22 above Sarah Cuttle; 22 below © Simon Bisset; 23 MMGI/Marianne Majerus, designer: Thomasina Tarling; 24 Andrew Lawson; 25 © MMGI Marianne Majerus, designers: Lynne Marcus and John Hall; 27 © Simon Bisset; 29 above © Simon Bisset; 29 below Thomas Hoblyn Garden Design; 31-35 above © Simon Bisset; 35 below Red House Television Limited; 36-39 © Simon Bisset; 41 John Carey/ Mainstreamimages; 42 © Simon Bisset; 43 above Red House Television Limited; 43 below Ian Kitson Landscape Architecture and Garden Design; 45 © Simon Bisset; 46 Matthew Wilson; 47 Jane Marika Smith; 48 © Simon Bisset; 49 above © Simon Bisset; 49 below Matthew Wilson; 51-53 © Simon Bisset; 54 above ©MMGI/Marianne Majerus, designer: Adam Caplin; 54 below Neil Sutherland/The Garden Collection; 55 Sarah Cuttle; 56 Nicola Stocken Tomkins/The Garden Collection; 57 Sarah Cuttle; 58 © Simon Bisset; 59 above Red House Television Limited; 59 below Jill FenwickInspired Garden Design; 61- 65 above © Simon Bisset; 65 below Matthew Wilson; 66-68 © Simon Bisset; 69 all © Simon Bisset, apart from 69 below right Jane Marika Smith; 70-71© Simon Bisset; 74 © Andrea Jones/private garden, London; 75 Nicola Stocken Tomkins/The Garden Collection; 76 GAP Photos/Suzie Gibbons; 77Nicola Stocken Tomkins/The Garden Collection; 78 above Ray Main/Mainstreamimages/domus furniture.co.uk; 78 below Steven Wooster/The Garden Collection, design: Laara Copley-Smith; 78-79 Clive Nichols/Charlotte Rowe; 81 Marcus Harpur/Saling Hall, Essex; 82 © Simon Bisset; 83 above Photolibrary.com; 83 below Marcus Harpur/Saling Hall, Essex; 84 Marcus Harpur, design: Justin Greer, London; 85 MMGI/Claire Takacs/King Johns Lodge, East Sussex, designers: Jill and Richard Cunningham; 87 above Steven Wooster/The Garden Collection, design: A. Green-Armytage/Garden World Images, design: Nava Habet; 87 below right Photolibrary.com; 88-89 Marcus Harpur, design: Judith Sharpe, London; 90 Jerry Harpur/design: Judith Sharpe, London; 91Marie O'Hara/The Garden Collection, The Little Cottage, Lymington; 92 Matthew Wilson; 93 Jerry Harpur/design: Simon Fraser, London; 95 Jane Marika Smith; 97 Andre Wood/Red Cover/Getty Images; 98 above Nicola Stocken Tomkins/The Garden Collection; 98 below Matthew Wilson; 98-99 © MMGI /Marianne Majerus, designer: Declan Buckley; 100 © Andrea Jones/Hermannshof Garden (Schau-und Sichtungsgarten Hermannshof), Germany; 101 Jerry Harpur, design: Lisette Pleasance, London; 103 Jane Marika Smith; 104 Steven Wooster/The Garden Collection, design: Louise del Balzo; 105 above © Andrea Jones/Evening Island. Chicago Botanic Garden.USA/Landscape Architecture and planting by Lisa E. Delplace OVSLA; 105 below left Nicola Stocken Tomkins/The Garden Collection, St Mary's Grove; 105 below right ©Living Etc/Paul Raeside/IPC+ Syndication; 106-107 Jane Marika Smith; 109 above left Jerry Harpur, design: Helen Dillon, Dublin; 109 above right Jane Marika Smith; 109 below left Andrew Lawson/The Dillon Garden, Dublin; 109 below right Liz Eddison/The Garden Collection, design: Cleve West, RHS Chelsea 2008; 111 MMGI/Marianne Majerus/Hermannshof, Weinheim, Germany, designer: Cassian Schmidt; 112-113 background Jane Marika Smith;112 inset above & below Jane Marika Smith;113 inset Jane Marika Smith; 114 Samantha Rolfe; 115 Greg Ryan/Sally Beyer/Red Cover/Getty Images; 117 Matthew Wilson; 119 above left © Simon Bisset; 119 above right Jane Marika Smith; 119 centre left © Andrea Jones/ The Westland Garden RHS Chelsea Flower Show 2007; Diarmuid Gavin & Stephen Reilly; 119 below left Lee Beel Photography; 119 below right Jane Marika Smith; 120-121 background Jane Marika Smith; 120 above inset Jane Marika Smith; 120 centre inset GAP Photos/Marg Cousens; 120 below inset Lee Beel Photography; 121 above & below inset Jane Marika Smith; 122-123 Jane Marika Smith; 124 Jerry Harpur/design: Ursel Gut, Bremen, Germany; 125 above © MMGI/Marianne Majerus, designer: Joe Swift; 125 below Wildscape/Alamy; 126 left © Andrea Jones/ Private coastal garden, Santa Barbara, California, design: Isabelle Greene Associates; 126 right Liz Eddison/The Garden Collection, design: Kate Gould, RHS Chelsea 07; 127 above © Simon Bisset/Thomas Hoblyn Garden;127 below John Carey/Main-streamimages; 129 Jane Marika Smith; 130 Sarah Cuttle; 131 GAP Photos/Andrea Jones; 132 Liz Eddison/The Garden Collection, design: Tom Stuart-Smith, RHS Chelsea 08; 133 T. sims/Garden World Images; 134 Nicola Stocken Tomkins/The Garden Collection, East Ruston Old Vicarage, Norfolk; 135 above © Simon Bisset/Great Dixter Gardens; 135 below Marcus Harpur/Saling Hall, Essex; 137 Andy Hay (rspb-images.com); 139 Jerry Harpur/design: David Stevens; 140 above Botanica/Photolibrary.com; 140 below © MMGI/Marianne Majerus; 141 Sarah Cuttle; 142-143 Photolibrary.com; 149 Matthew Wilson; 151 Thomas Hoblyn Garden Design; 152 Helen Fickling (Design: Thomas Hoblyn)/RHS Chelsea Flower Show 2009; 153 © Simon Bisset/Thomas Hoblyn Garden; 154-155 Clive Nichols/Charlotte Rowe; 156-157 © MMGI/Marianne Majerus; 158-159 Clive Nichols/Lisette Pleasance; 160-161 Clive Nichols; 162-185 Matthew Wilson; 186-187 © Simon Bisset.

For Jane, Dylan and Amelie, with love.

First published in 2009 by
Quadrille Publishing Limited
Alhambra House
27–31 Charing Cross Road
London WC2H 0LS
www.quadrille.co.uk

For the book
Editorial Director Jane O'Shea
Art Director Helen Lewis
Project Editor Simon Davis
Designer David Rowley
Picture Research Samantha Rolfe
Special Photography Simon Bisset
Production Director Vincent Smith
Production Controller Ruth Deary

For the television series
Creative Director John Silver
Series Editor Simon Bisset
Directors Matthew Cox and Ed St Giles
Assistant Producers Nicks Bullard and Louisa Macinnes
Production Manager Lotta Hellzen

ISBN 978 184400 762 2

Printed and bound in Germany

GOOD WOOD
FINISHES